# THE
# DIGNITY
# DIET

## HOW TO END THE CYCLE OF
## CRY-EAT-REP*EAT*

LIN M. ELEOFF, JD

DISCLAIMER: The material contained herein is intended as a reference volume only and not as a medical manual. This book is intended to help you make informed decisions when it comes to your emotional and physical well-being.

ISBN-13: 978-0983286806
ISBN-10: 0983286809

Library of Congress Control Number: 2011900927
Lin M. Eleoff
Barrington, RI

Printed in the United States of America

# THE
# DIGNITY
# DIET

This book is dedicated to Eda Eleoff
with love,
always and forever.

# Table of Contents

# Acknowledgments

I am forever indebted to all the women who have allowed me into their lives, trusting me with their precious stories. It has been an incredible honor and privilege to be able to work with such amazingly brave women; together we have rewritten some powerful stories. My heartfelt thanks go out to each and every one of them.

This book would still be in rough draft form on my computer if not for Brooke Castillo who lovingly pushed and prodded me to get it finished. Thank you, dear Brooke. I love it when you push me around.

I want to give a loud and boisterous shout-out to Cookie, Katie, Kris, Deb, Suyin, Sarah, C. J., and Bev for the ride of a lifetime (including that zip-line ride through the redwoods of Napa). Thank you all for your love, support, feedback, and most importantly, your special brand of awesomeness.

I wish to acknowledge the never-ending love, support, encouragement, and ass kicking from my BB&LLF, Mary. I love you, girlie. Thank you for believing in me.

I would be remiss if I didn't acknowledge my brother. Mark, even though you had absolutely nothing to do with the writing of this book, I know how much you love seeing your name in print. I love you. You bug me. I couldn't ask for a better brother.

Thank you, beautiful Corinne. I hereby pronounce you my sister (Why waste time on technicalities?). I love you with all my heart. You lift me up.

Thank you, Moots, for everything that you do for me, for your unconditional love, steadfast support, and remarkable resilience. You have taught me so much, my dearest, most wonderful mother—you truly are the rock beneath my feet.

I have been blessed with four beautiful children: Brooklin, Dylan, MacKenzie, and Rhianon. I would have to write a whole other book to properly acknowledge them for all that they mean to me. Thank you, my precious ones, for your patience and understanding during those times when I was buried in my writing. Each of you inspires me to new heights. My heart swells with love for you.

And finally, to Stephen, my most amazing husband—no one loves me like you do. I thank you for believing in me, waiting for me, waiting *on* me, and for being there, always. You are my rock. I love you, Thurston. And I love being your Lovey.

I am overflowing with gratitude.

# INTRODUCTION:
# SO YOU WANT TO LOSE
# WEIGHT? PROVE IT

Talk is cheap. It's always on sale. And it never runs out.

In short, *talk is fattening* when all you do is talk.

How much you weigh has a lot to do with your own special brand of "talk"; especially the way you talk to your Self. Too much talk and not enough walk makes for an ever-expanding backside.

Have you heard yourself talk to your *Self* lately?

## YOU, YOURSELF, AND YOUR *SELF*—THERE'S A DIFFERENCE

You'll notice that at various times throughout this book I make the distinction between yourself and your Self. When I use the word "Self" with a capital, I'm referring to your whole Self, which includes little-y you—the part of you that has been socialized and programed in ways that don't always serve your best interests (and yes, of course, there are many times when that programming absolutely serves you well).

Think of your Self as the umbrella that encompasses and knows all the parts of who You (with a capital Y) ultimately are: it's the *dignified* part of you that inherently knows that you are worthy, you are enough, and you matter, no matter what.

Your Self is also part of a greater whole that we all belong to—the Universe. That is why I sometimes refer to "our *Self*." Although it may not be grammatically correct, it is a distinction that I consider important and helpful in understanding who we are as individuals; that we are each integral parts of something we can't even fully comprehend.

Your Self, I believe, is the compass that will lead you back to your Dignity and keep you in Integrity, but only to the extent that you are aware of and believe in your unequivocal worth as a human being.

Just because you (the small 'y' version) may not believe in your incalculable value to the entire Universe, doesn't mean your Self agrees. Your Self *knows*, in the deepest sense of that word, how valuable you are, even when you say things like:

- I really should lose weight.
- This weight has got to come off.
- I need to go on a diet.
- I'm starting tomorrow.
- I want another donut.
- I can't believe I just ate all the donuts.
- I can't believe how much weight I've gained.
- I'll have fries with that.
- I have to lose weight for the wedding.
- I'm definitely going to fit into a bikini this summer.
- I cannot resist food.
- I don't know why this keeps happening.

- I'll start tomorrow.
- Can you please pass the cookies?
- Why did you bring cookies in the house? You know I can't eat them!
- No, really, this time I'm starting tomorrow.
- For sure, no matter what, I am going to start watching what I eat. Tomorrow.
- I have to lose twenty pounds by Saturday.
- Are you going to eat all that?

And these are just some of the things you say *on a good day.*

On the not-so-good days it's probably more like:

- I ruined everything.
- There's something wrong with me.
- I am such a loser.
- This is too hard for me to handle.
- I have no willpower.
- I'm an idiot.
- Shoot me now.

You may believe all your mean talk, but your Self knows better. She's just waiting for you to listen to *her* side of the story—the side without the "sob" in front of it.

When you stop to think about it—I mean really think about it— we tend to do a whole lot of talking and not a lot of doing, at least not the kind of doing that will get us what we say we want.

We talk about wanting to lose weight, and then we don't do the things that naturally lead to weight loss.

Why? Why would we say one thing and do (or not do) another?

This book is going to shed a big bright light on all the ways you sabotage yourself (your true Self cannot be sabotaged, by the way), and *why* you do what you do. Understanding the "why" behind your actions (in particular, when it comes to overeating) will give you great insight into why you aren't actually losing weight and keeping it off. You see, it's not enough to just lose the weight; you've got to have Integrity when you lose it, or it'll come right back. When you lose weight without Integrity it means you didn't bother to get your Self to buy in—you are miserable when you start and, even if you do manage to lose the weight, you'll be miserable in the end. After all, as they say, an unhappy journey will never lead you to a happy ending. In this book I'm (strongly) positing that in order to lose weight with Integrity (and therefore keep it off) you've got to take care of your Self *first*. Your Self will always lead you on a happy journey.

Overweight is a symptom of an underlying state of inner anarchy, an overall sense of dissatisfaction without a deep understanding of what's causing the dissatisfaction. This is why all those efforts to stop overeating never actually solve the problem—they're merely tricks you've been playing on yourself in a desperate effort to treat the symptom by changing the behavior.

Silly rabbit.

You can't do that without having your Self fight you back. Your Self is allergic to unhappy journeys. She's also looking for some respect, and you might want to think about giving it to her because you really could use her help. In short, without your Self on board, the struggle in your mind will continue. She will always call you out on your BS. Eating food is just a way to ignore her.

Without identifying the root cause of *why* you overeat (it's different for everyone), you will eventually go back to overeating. That's because your mind has programmed itself to eat to feel better, even when your body isn't hungry.

Do you know why you *over*eat?

What's the *feeling* that food helps you ignore?

What's the feeling you want to avoid? Have you ever thought to ask your body what it needs instead of giving your mind what it thinks it wants?

Can you feel the mental and emotional struggle?

There's a disconnect somewhere. Our job is to find the disconnect and then *reconnect*. The disconnect happens when you stop paying attention to your Self and your fantastically brilliant body. We tend to want to blame our bodies when the real culprit is our mind, which can be one giant pain in the ass. It talks *a lot*. And it drags our bodies along, kicking and screaming.

Meanwhile, your Self refuses to walk that talk. It knows when the mind has lost its Dignity.

Dignity is everything. As in—

Every.

Thing.

Dignity burns calories with ease. Dignity doesn't require willpower. Dignity is what connects the mind to the body and ultimately to the Self, that part of you that transcends mere talk. Your Self knows where you lost your Dignity, and if you pay attention, she will help you find it again.

The only other thing you need to "complete the look" is Integrity. Dignity plus Integrity creates a one-two punch that causes fat to drip off the body faster than you can say, "Please sir, I want more."

The Dignity Diet will teach you how to look at your life from thirty thousand feet above thought level. Thought level is where the mind is allowed to chatter away at will. The effects of such chatter are evident in each of the various aspects of your life, including your physical health and well-being.

In short, the Dignity Diet is so much better for you than the White-Knuckle Diet. Whereas the White Knuckle Diet relies solely on willpower to force you to change your deeply ingrained eating habits, the Dignity Diet is all about using your *willingness power* to feed your body and your Self exactly what they need. The Dignity Diet teaches the mind to fall in line behind your Self; your Self transcends your mind's ability to merely think.

Your Self *knows.*

In fact, your Self possesses a deep knowing of the sacredness of who You are and the space you inhabit in the Universe. Your Self is due for a promotion. Your mind, meanwhile, probably needs a (loving) kick in the ass.

# PART 1

# The Heroine's Journey through the Four Stages of Weight Loss

*As you embark on your journey remember this: Your only real purpose in life is to figure out a way to take care of your Self first— to take full responsibility for your life—so that you can show up big and strong and authentic for those you love the most.*

## THE HEROINE'S JOURNEY

Pack your bags, because you're going on a perilous adventure into the unknown. Destiny has summoned you (the heroine) to a place of unimaginable torment and exquisite delight. The pay-off? Your Dignity, baby.

It's not enough to just *say* you want something. You also have to prove it, or you don't really want it badly enough to make it

Are you ready to get your Dignity back?

Want to lose weight?

Prove it!

# STAGE 1

# Refusing the Call to Adventure or "The Last Thing I Need Is <u>A</u>nother <u>F</u>#%&ing <u>G</u>rowth <u>O</u>pportunity"

## HOW "AFGO AVOIDANCE" PACKS ON THE POUNDAGE

Your struggle with weight is an AFGO—Another F#%&ing Growth Opportunity—a call to adventure like no other. Think of an AFGO as an invitation from the Universe to go on a journey to reclaim your Dignity. Dignity is *everything*. Without it we create a life that's messier than a lasagna sandwich—a mirror image of the mess inside our heads.

Here's how to know you've received an AFGO invite: you'll have "that certain feeling" (a familiar sensation you know only too well) that tells you something isn't quite right in your world. Your Self is trying to tell you something, and you aren't listening. You're too busy fighting against the feeling. You may not even realize the feeling is happening because you're so used to it that it feels "normal."

It's that feeling you get when you feel stupid.

Or ignored.

Or disrespected.

Or bullied.

Or invalidated.

Or fat.

None of those is actually a physical feeling. For example, "fat" isn't a feeling. But if you're someone who is easily triggered into "feeling fat," you know *exactly* what it feels like. Maybe your chest feels tight or your head feels light or your throat feels constricted. Or maybe it's that kick in the gut feeling you experienced when you got fired, or when he left you, or when she said she hated you, or when you saw your reflection in the mirror.

That feeling (hopeless, perhaps?) is your big fat clue that an AFGO is knocking at your door. And you're not answering.

Welcome to stage 1 where AFGOs are not welcome. And no wonder, really, because AFGOs are a galactic pain in the posterior, no matter how big or small your posterior happens to be. They require that you pay attention to your Self, that you put your Self first. That's not a priority when you're stuck in stage 1, where your Self is often relegated to the backseat.

An AFGO is a signal we receive from our Self that something isn't sitting right with us. The Self speaks to us through the body, so the signal is experienced as an emotion we typically do not want to feel. Not wanting to feel our feelings, besides being great fodder for skits on *Saturday Night Live*, can lead to doing things that make us feel better in the moment (cookie, anyone?) but ultimately fix nothing. We let the AFGO slip away. We turn down the call to adventure, but not without consequences, because refusing the call means we stay stuck in stage 1 for all of eternity (hyperbole duly noted but admittedly intended for shock value).

When we fail to deal with our AFGOs we are out of Integrity. We overeat despite having made the promise to ourselves that we were going to "be good." The reason we step out of Integrity is because we haven't yet reclaimed our Dignity.

## THE HEROINE'S JOURNEY (WHERE *YOU* ARE THE HEROINE)

You've no doubt received the call to adventure several times before but have chosen to pass on the opportunity, perhaps because an AFGO is an invitation that often feels like a smack to the upside of the head. It's no wonder you might choose to ignore it.

In actuality, an AFGO is a gift that keeps on giving (and re-giving!) until you learn the lesson that it's there to teach you about You. After all, your purpose in life, your only real purpose, is to figure out a way to take care of your Self first so that you can show up big and strong and authentic for the world. It's the best kind of *Selfish*. Everyone in your world wins. There are triple karma points earned when you put your Self first in this way.

The reality we create on a daily basis, in each of the various aspects of our lives, is a reflection of whether we're taking full advantage of those AFGO invitations or, instead, we're letting them pass us by. After all, an AFGO isn't exactly an invitation to a fancy schmancy ball; on the contrary, it's more like an invite to a party of lions, tigers, and bears. Oh my!

And still—you should go.

Unless you'd rather keep the blinders on and refuse to take responsibility for creating happiness in *all* aspects of your life, preferring instead to put that task on the people (your mom), places (your job), and things (food) that show up in your life and "make" you feel powerless. Oh, I know you don't mean to do that, but if you're like so many of the women I've coached, you keep choosing the path of least resistance only to find that it never really leads to *lasting* happiness. That's a whole different kind of happiness—Self created happiness is *soooooooooo* worth trekking through perilous terrain to attain, but only if you believe with all your heart that you are worth it.

## ENDING THE PERILOUS CYCLE OF CRY-EAT-REP*EAT*

An AFGO starts out as a whisper in builds to a very loud knock at the door. Its purpose is to call attention to the parts of your life that are weighing you down, literally (your heavy body) and figuratively (your heavy head). You can choose to answer the knock or stay stuck in an endless and rather risky cycle of Cry-Eat-Repeat. When you're in stage 1, you're oblivious to the knock. You're using food like earplugs. Food keeps you from feeling the feeling you don't want to feel. Notice it's not Cry-*Feel*-Repeat;

that's because you don't want to feel the feeling—eating allows you to pretend it's not there. *Feeling? What feeling?*

We cry because we hurt, but instead of trying to understand why we're hurting, we eat. Then we cry because of the guilt we invariably feel, so we say, "Screw it," and then rep*eat*.

Ultimately we use this merry-go-round cycle of Cry-Eat-Rep*eat* as further evidence that we'll "never lose weight."

If you've been struggling with your weight for a long time, it may be time to start paying attention to the knock because there's an AFGO calling and you're avoiding it, Mama.

Worrying, obsessing, and stressing about weight is what an undignified mind does on autopilot. It's enough to make you want to eat the whole thing—and then some. Understanding stage 1 and why you've been refusing the call to adventure for so long is crucial to ending the cycle of Cry-Eat-Rep*eat*.

I know you say you want to lose weight, but there's something else you want, and you want it more than anything else in the world, but you're not getting it. You think losing weight will give it to you. You believe a smaller ass is the ticket to feeling happy. In other words, you believe you have to *wait* to be happy. You believe you have to wait until happiness comes *to you* in the form of a smaller ass.

But what if—just go with me on this—what if it's the other way around? What if the key to having an incredibly shrinking ass is to find a way to get said ass to Happy, *now*? *Read that sentence again* because, if you're entrenched in stage 1, you'll want to gloss right over it—you'll want to pretend I didn't just say that. You'll tell yourself that it's a bunch of bunk. And *that* kind of thinking,

Unhappiness is fattening. Your AFGO, should you choose to accept it, is to figure out the ways you're creating unhappiness in your life, which causes you to want to eat to feel better. Figure that out, deal with what's causing the struggle, and then watch what happens. Be prepared to amaze yourself.

## IDENTIFYING YOUR FATTENING THINK-FEEL-DO HABIT LOOPS

When it comes to your weight, your mind has been programmed to think a certain way. As long as you continue to think this way, you will stay stuck in stage 1. It can be no other way. That's because the way you think affects the way you feel. Feelings determine what you do (or don't do), and your behavior ultimately creates an outcome, and all those outcomes add up to create your reality.

Think → Feel → Do → Outcome → Reality

If your outcome is weight gain and your reality is an overweight body, then the "do" part of the equation, the action or behavior, has been to overeat. Working backward, action is driven by feelings: we act in accordance with the way we feel. Therefore, if the "feeling" part of the equation is negative in any way, then you're likely eating to feed your hungry mind, even if your body is not hungry. What's your mind hungry for? Well, apparently, it's hungry for *another* feeling, and it thinks food is the answer because the feeling that comes with eating food is better than the other feeling you don't want to feel.

Have you noticed how easy it is to pass on food when you're feeling happy and in love? Wouldn't it be great if you could feed your Self more happiness and love instead of donuts and French fries? What if you could fall in love with your Self? Because up to now the love that your Self has had for you has been unrequited.

So, here's the tricky question: What's the (negative) feeling that causes you to seek comfort in food? Is it boredom? Loneliness? Frustration? Helplessness? Stress?

Is it sadness? Anger? Ambivalence? Panic?

What is it? This isn't a trick question, but it is a *tricky* question to answer. In fact, for many people who've been struggling with their weight for a very long time, it's extremely difficult to answer because they've never paid attention to the feeling long enough to name it. They haven't wanted to pay attention to it because they don't like feeling the feeling, whatever it may be. They just want it to stop.

Enter *food*.

Food has been given the job of making you feel better. It's a quick, albeit temporary, fix.

And it's a very convenient way to ignore the AFGO.

It's enough to make a grown woman cry.

Then eat to feel better.

Then feel badly for eating.

Then cry all over again for being such a loser in all the wrong ways.

Repeat.

Damn. Stage 1 really *sssssuuuuuuuuuuuuuuuucks.*

**⊄D**

Stage 1 is home to the Cry-Eat-Repeat cycle that makes you feel like you're stuck between a double-glazed chocolate donut and a hard place. In stage 1 you have very little awareness of your TFD habits. You go through your day, thinking and feeling and doing, on autopilot. All you can see is that there's a whole lot of crying, eating, and repeating going on.

Of course, stage 1 is different for everyone, but the common ground is this: the attention given to food and eating is out of proportion to the attention given to your whole life. What's most ironic is that you probably think overeating is the problem. But overeating is a *symptom* of unhappiness somewhere in your life, not the cause of it. Finding the actual cause is the work you'll be doing in this book, and, once again, that requires looking at your life as a whole

## AFGO SPOTTING: "BUT IT JUST TASTES SO GOOD, I CAN'T RESIST"

Let's start with a common AFGO that is relatively easy to spot: it's triggered by an event such as the sudden appearance of cake (for example) at the office. You believe you "can't resist" the cake.

A belief is a thought that's had a lot of practice. We tend to think of beliefs as *facts.* We believe that not being able to resist certain foods is a fact of life and there's nothing that can be done to change it (or, at least, nothing we can think of).

Here's a thought you can think: "Maybe it's not true that I can't resist cake."

That's your growth opportunity—your AFGO: to challenge the Self limiting belief that you are a helpless and hopeless mess when it comes to the taste of foods you love to eat. That is a very fattening lie, dear reader. Get ready to put it to the test.

Maybe it's not true.

Maybe it's not true.

Maybe it's not true.

Make this your mantra as you get better and better at spotting your AFGOs. Changing our beliefs is challenging work. That's why we start with *"maybe* it's not true."

## THE TRIGGERING EVENT

AFGO spotting requires an open mind. Stage 1, however, is not exactly known for open-mindedness when it comes to the things we choose to believe about our bodies, our weight, and the food we eat. Taking full advantage of those AFGOs requires a willingness to look at things differently in order to produce a different outcome: weight loss that is a natural consequence of taking care of your Self.

Welcoming your AFGOs automatically expands your mind: it opens the doors to a whole new way of thinking, feeling, and doing your life. You'll know an AFGO has presented itself because you'll feel a familiar pang in your throat, your chest, or your gut caused by a triggering event. A triggering event is unique to

15

you; it's a circumstance—a person, place, or thing—that triggers a predictable and typical Think-Feel-Do response in you. Someone else may respond to the circumstance in an entirely different way; someone else may not even notice the person, place, or *cake* that has triggered you.

That's why it is an AFGO. Its purpose is to show you how the way you think (and feel and do) is limiting your right to create and experience joy. You are, in effect, blocking your own happiness. WTF?

No really—*What The Fuuuuuuuuuuuuuuuuuuuuuuuu...?*

Why would you block your own happiness?

Hmmmm—let me see...

Because YOU'RE IN STAGE 1. The hallmark of stage 1 is being unaware of all the ways that you're blocking your own happiness.

Once again, that's what AFGOs are for—to show you how you're giving away your happiness, at great cost to your Self. The first step is to be able to spot an AFGO. You've probably become so adept at pushing them aside, you may not know one when it hits you. This might help: you're more likely to sniff out an AFGO by the way it makes you *feel*. Hint: it'll be some version of "lousy." That lousy feeling, if you pay attention to it, will allow you to identify the thought that started you down the road of "lousy." You will then begin to understand why you *do* the lousy things you do. When possible, see if you can also identify the underlying beliefs that support this lousy way of thinking by asking yourself why you believe your thoughts.

To help you identify your counterproductive Think-Feel-Do habits, fill out this worksheet whenever you spot an AFGO.

## AFGO SPOTTING EXERCISE

Triggering Event (Person, Place, or Thing):

What do I *feel* when I get triggered in this way?

Why do I feel this way? (This will give you the *thought* that drives the feeling.)

What do I *do* when I think and feel this way?

What underlying *beliefs* do I have that support this thought? (Why do you think this way?)

Here's the thing: you cannot see what you are *not willing* to see. Even as you read the words on this page, the thoughts in your head may be pushing back: *No way. That is soooooooo not the problem.* I understand that you believe that. But I wonder if you might be willing to clear your head just enough to drop all the thoughts and beliefs you've held on to so tightly for all these years, at least while you're reading this book. You can have them back. I promise I'm not trying to take anything from you. What I'd like to do is give you some food for thought (that pun was totally intended). I'd like to offer you another way to look at things. I want to show you what you may have been missing—what you've been unable or unwilling to see until now.

behavior without awareness of the thought processes that drive it.

You actually do have options, but believing you don't will most certainly lure you into a mind-set that causes you to feel even more stuck, and the behaviors that follow will be driven by that feeling of being stuck.

Often, the uncomfortable feeling of being stuck perpetuates the desire to eat to feel better. Until you uncover the mind-set, challenge it, test the theory upon which it's premised, and *then* decide if you're willing to change it, you won't be able to create lasting change in your whole life, not just your weight. Mind-sets absolutely can be changed. It starts with the realization that there is actually no external force at work trying to bring you down—you are in charge of your life. You can turn this steamboat around.

It's all on you, Mamacakes. That's a much more empowering way to think about it, don't you *think*? Right now, the only thing to focus on is the way you *think*. Stage 1 is *never* the time to eat less and exercise more. It's not the time to *do* anything. Doing anything when you're in stage 1 is going to require a lot of energy (willpower), and eventually you will burn out. Boom! You're back where you started.

Ugh! Is that any way to *be*?

If stage 1 is where your head's at, then first things first: let's get you a new head (kidding). Let's change what's going on *inside* your head. If you focus on losing the weight in your head, the weight on your body will naturally come off, no "trying" required. Notice I didn't say it will "melt" off; I said it would *naturally* come off. Besides, trying is all in your head. Which is why you must stop trying to do anything. Stop everything. Hold your horses. Put the brakes on.

Halt!

Slow down. This is a process, and if you're in the beginning stage, you are neither willing nor able to *do* anything when it comes to losing weight. This is a time for introspection and curiosity.

The first order of business is to acknowledge that you are indeed in stage 1 by proclaiming out loud, "I am in stage 1."

Go on. Say it. LOUDER! I suggest you not read any farther until you are willing to surrender to the reality of where you are in this moment.

"I am in stage 1."

"I am in stage 1."

"I am in stage 1."

If you have to, start reading again from the top.

Don't worry, I'll wait for you.

**◁▷**

*Aaaaaaaaaaand* we're back. Great. Hopefully you're willingly beginning to surrender to stage 1. That's awesome. Now, be prepared to forget everything you've just learned. Insert deep breath here because your mind, which is addicted to roller coaster rides, is going to fight to take you back to denial because that's what it knows. You've been *think*ing and *feel*ing and *doing* things a certain way for a very long time. Old habits die hard, especially our old TFD habits. So even though you may acknowledge today that you are indeed in stage 1, be prepared to have to remind yourself over and over again tomorrow. Put sticky notes on the refrigerator, on the bathroom mirror, and even on the dog's tail. Create a reminder on your smart phone. Write "I am in stage 1" with a Sharpie on the palm of your hand. Rent a billboard.

If you could see my face right now, you'd know that I am not kidding.

Awareness is your golden ticket to stage 2. When you acknowledge that you are in stage 1, it means that you're done with the old way even though you haven't yet learned the new way. You are preparing to enter the space between where you are today and where you ultimately want to be. Just as a caterpillar must spend time in a cocoon before it becomes a butterfly, so too must you create some space for your own transformation. This is where you will focus on taking care of you—especially the parts of you that you've been using food to take care of.

Hopefully you're starting to feel the load lift even slightly off your shoulders. Your knuckles should be turning pink again. There's a reason you haven't been able to figure this out: you've been running the same old program in your mind. It's that programming that always steers you back to food, ignoring your body's hunger and satiety signals.

At this point you probably have no idea what tricks your mind has been playing on you. That's OK. For now, the best thing you can do is *exhale*. If you have a white piece of cloth, wave it around. Surrender. If you happen to spot an AFGO, cool. If not, that's OK too.

It's hard to admit that we haven't taken care of our physical health. It's easier to pretend there "must be some other reason" why things are the way they are today. But the real reason is that you haven't been paying attention to your mind, and when you don't, your mind has a way of doing the opposite of what your heart desires.

The really good news is this: once you're willing to take back control of your mind so that you can help your Self, you can absolutely have what your heart desires. If you're willing to slow it down enough to give your Self the gift of your full attention, then you will succeed in your efforts to lose weight. As you will learn, willingness is a key ingredient in your recipe for success.

So, if you've stopped kicking and screaming, if you've decided to now accept the AFGO invitation to go on your Heroine's Journey, then you are finally ready for stage 2: initiation.

## READY TO MOVE ON TO STAGE 2?

Use the following checklist to determine whether you're ready for stage 2. Unless you can check them all, go back and review stage 1 before moving ahead.

- ☐ You're so damn sick of the White-Knuckle Diet.

- ☐ You're waving the white flag of surrender.

- ☐ You realize it's your heavy head that's weighing you down.

- ☐ You're beginning to see that you may have unwittingly become a prisoner of your own mind.

- ☐ Enough already with the crying, eating, and repeating— you're done!

# STAGE 2

# Initiation or "Does This Thought Make My Butt Look Fat?"

## HOW THE WAY YOU THINK AFFECTS THE SIZE OF YOUR ASS

To the uninitiated, being overweight is the one thing that is blocking their happiness. Ergo, losing weight is The Solution to The Problem.

But if this were true, then *all* thin people would be happy and problem free. If you are not thin and you believe thinness is the Holy Grail that must be pursued at all costs, you may be stuck in the crosshairs between stages 1 and 2: you want things to change but, then again, you don't.

Here's how you'll know: your mind will be insisting with all its might that you "have to lose weight, *or else*____" (fill in the blank). It's really important that you pause here and fill in that blank because that's the shiitake that's holding you back. For example, if you believe that you "have to lose weight in order to be at peace," that's the thought that creates a feeling of helplessness that makes you want to scarf down the closest thing resembling food. You create the feeling of helplessness in your mind, and then you turn to food because you don't like feeling helpless. Your overweight body doesn't cause you to feel helpless; it's how you think about your body that creates the feeling of helplessness.

Think "My miserable body makes me feel horrible"→Feel helpless→Eat to feel better (eat to feed your mind).

Instead:

Think "I am at peace"→Feel at peace→Eat only to feed your body, not your mind.

Counterintuitive? Absolutely. The mind can be crazy cuckoo nuts. It talks in circles, creates nonsense, and looks to blame anything and anyone else for the havoc it creates. Even if your ass is actually fat, you still want someone to tell you it's not. Check out this conversation I had recently with a woman named Anna:

Anna: *If my husband loved me, he wouldn't tell me my ass is fat.*

Me: *Why did he tell you your ass is fat?*

Anna: *Because I asked him if he thought it was.*

Me: *Do you think your ass is fat?*

Anna: *Yes. Obviously it is.*

Me: *And what do you want him to think?*

Anna: *I just want him to love me no matter what.*

Me: *Do you love you no matter what?*

Anna: *Not when my ass looks like this.*

Me: *Does your husband love you?*

Anna: *Yes, he really does. I know he does.*

Me: *Even when your ass is fat?*

Anna: *Yup.*

Me: *Interesting.*

That's how we abdicate responsibility for our emotional well-being: we talk in circles. We expect others to play an emotional mind game with us just so we can feel good about ourselves, even though it doesn't work. Anna didn't want to know if her husband thought her ass was fat (she already knew it was), she just wanted reassurance that he loved her, even though she knew he did. She set him up so that she could beat herself up and blame it on him.

Incidentally, if an ass looks like it's fat, moves like it's fat, and requires bigger pants, we have to at least consider the possibility that it is indeed fat.

But we don't need to make it mean anything more than that. To do so is colossally counterproductive to the task at hand, which is—all together now—learning to take responsibility for the way we think so that we can feel better and then do better.

How we *think* affects the way we *feel*. How we feel affects what we *do*.

Think crappy thoughts. Feel like crap. Eat crap to feel better. Create a crappy fat ass.

Why would we expect anything else?

## YOUR ONE HUNDRED POUND HEAD

Have you ever wondered how much a thought weighs? I have. (These are the things I find so fascinating.) I think of thoughts as having *weight*. Some thoughts are light and airy—they lift us up. Others are, well, heavy and burdensome—they pull us down, down, *down*.

The next question is this: How much does your head weigh? We spend so much time focusing on how much our bodies weigh, but I think it's the weight in our heads that weighs us down and causes us to eat, and that's why we gain weight. That's why I think it's more important to know how much your head weighs.

The actual weight of a normal head is about eleven pounds, a trivial piece of information in the context of this discussion, but I thought you might want to know. What's relevant here is how heavy your head *feels*. If your head feels heavy, then something's gotta give, and don't be surprised if it's your hips and thighs.

Your head is home to billions of thoughts—way too many for you to be aware of in any given moment. Each of those thoughts has an impact on you, whether you're aware of it or not. If your body is overweight, pay attention to your head first, because I'm guessing it feels like it weighs one hundred pounds.

Give or take.

While you've been focusing on the weight of your body, your head has been getting fatter and fatter, and it's the worst kind of fat: the invisible kind. The kind that makes you want to—you know—cry, eat, and repeat. And that just makes your butt look fat. This is good news. Knowing that the body you have today is a reflection of the way you think is fantastic news because you have the ability to change the way you think. You can choose a whole new set of thoughts and beliefs that lighten the load in your head. If you lose the invisible fat in your head, the actual fat on your body will disappear. There won't be anything to make it stay.

As much as you might want to blame your body for being over-weight, it's not your body's "fault." Your body is doing the only thing it can do: process the food you keep feeding it even when it doesn't need food. Your body has been made a slave to what's going on in your head. Your head, meanwhile, has become an expert at convincing you that food will make "it" all better, what-ever "it" is.

Isn't it time you poked around inside your noggin to find out exactly what's happening in there? Or does the fear of what you may find inside hold you back?

## YOUR MIND IS A PARADOX

Your mind is a paradox when, like your body, it ought to be a won-derland. It should be working *for* you because the way you feel is your mind's responsibility. If you want a smaller ass, take respon-sibility for how your mind *thinks* so that you can *feel* inspired to *do* whatever it takes to make it happen.

You *say* you want to lose weight, but—hear this—you also *don't* want to lose weight, because losing weight represents something difficult or painful. It feels like deprivation; or perhaps it feels like you're about to lose the one thing that gives you comfort: food. Well, is it any wonder you don't really want to lose weight? In your mind, losing weight has become something difficult and painful; of course you're not going to feel motivated to take action when you think this way. It makes perfect sense. Your fattening thoughts are causing you to "feel" fat, and when you feel fat you don't want to deal—with anything.

The lesson of stage 2 is this: the reason you haven't been able to lose weight and keep it off is because of the mixed messages your mind keeps sending out:

*You have to eat less, exercise more.* → Don't bother, what's the point? →*Stop eating so much!* → Who cares? It's no use. → *You're in big trouble now.* → But I can't resist.

Whoa, Cowgirl! That's a lot of mixed-up messaging, and it's all coming from one source: your mind. It's time your mind and your Self got on the same page, don't you think?

**⊄⊃**

People don't often take the time to really think about how their mind *thinks* and what it *believes* and the choices that are made as a result. If you're tempted to skip ahead and "just get on with the diet" part of this book, then you're not quite ready for stage 2, let alone part 2 of this book. You're not ready to get over your own mind. If that's the case, go back and read stage 1. Notice the resistance that your mind is using to fight against your Self—the part of you that knows better.

If you're eating junk food it's because you're thinking undignified thoughts—thoughts that are damaging to your Self esteem and make you feel powerless. Believe undignified thoughts at your peril.

*Undignified thoughts* are demotivating and lead to undignified behavior that you later regret.

*Dignified thoughts* motivate and inspire you to make choices you are proud of.

Undignified thoughts are those you think without thinking; they're the *thought habits* that are in your mind that create a *feeling habit* of powerlessness, which leads to an *action habit* of overeating.

Junk thoughts include:

- There's no use.
- This is hopeless.
- I'm such a loser.
- I give up.
- I'm sick of this.
- I'm disgusting.
- My body is gross.
- I'll never lose weight.
- There's something wrong with me.
- I'm so embarrassed.
- People are going to think I'm lazy and pathetic.

Junky and undignified thoughts run in the background of your subconscious mind where they're not technically "thoughts" because you're not aware that they're even there. Nevertheless, each (subconscious) thought you think has a ripple effect through-out your body, much like a pebble causes a series of concentric waves when thrown into the water. Your thought vibrations are "felt" by the cells in your body, which means the health of your body is greatly influenced by the thoughts you think without thinking. Indeed, as Deepak Chopra says, "There is no difference between a thought and a molecule in the brain."

*Think* Habit → *Feel* Habit → *Do* Habit → Same ol' Reality

Junk thought habits are a lot like junk food; they lead to undignified outcomes—the ones you're *not* happy with.

Dignified thought habits lead to dignified outcomes—the ones that make you happy and proud.

If you're ready to move forward, if you're starting to get curious about what's going on in your noggin, then take some time to really think about how you would complete the following sentences. No matter how difficult, it's important that you bring your thoughts and beliefs to the forefront of your conscious mind because that's where your power to change is.

If I never lose weight, then…

If I never lose weight, it will mean that I…

If I don't lose weight, I worry that…

If I don't lose weight, people will think…

Being overweight means that I am…

If I were to lose weight, it would mean that I…

If I were to lose weight, my life would…

If I were to lose weight, the people in my life would…

Your initiation into stage 2 is intended to help you realize that your overweight body is a *symptom* of your discontent, not the cause of it. Your overweight body is—drumroll please—just Another F#%&ing Growth Opportunity; it's an AFGO of mind-blowing proportions. There is so much personal growth to be gleaned from understanding your weight struggle.

Paying attention to the way you think is your focus in stage 2. Once you're willing to consider that it's your mind that's causing the expansion of your ass, it's time to start paying close attention to the running dialogue that spills forth from your mind on an almost constant basis. Without that awareness, real change is less likely to occur.

Before you continue reading, go back over your answers to the questions above. As a follow-up to each of your answers, ask yourself these questions:

- When did I learn to think this way? How old is this way of thinking?
- Where or from whom did I learn to think this way? Who and what were my early influencers?
- What if, *as an adult*, I questioned my own thinking? How might I challenge the thoughts I believe?
- How does thinking this way help me?
- How does thinking this way hurt and/or hinder me?
- Am I willing to put this thought "on hold" for now?

In the meantime, let's do some myth busting, shall we?

## THE D-MYTH

I know, I know, I keep hearing it, too: "Diets don't work." However, I respectfully disagree; I'm pretty certain that people *can* lose weight on a diet, whether it's a "sensible diet" or the all-you-can-eat-as-long-as-you-don't-really-eat "air diet" that some celebrities have actually proven *works*! If the goal is to lose weight, then even a cookie diet is going to "work" if you sufficiently restrict the number of cookie calories you consume on a daily basis.

The D-Myth—that diets don't work—is the latest message being touted to those already suffering from a severe case of diet mentality and it feeds right into an already self-destructive mind-set. Think about it: diet mentality is about the mind—the way we *think* about food and weight and our bodies. On the other hand, going "on a diet" is what we *do*... it's an action. This is an important distinction because the action (dieting) is driven by the thoughts a person is thinking—their mind-set. A woman whose mind-set is locked in diet mentality is going to create a totally different outcome for herself compared to a woman with a healthy mind-set, even if they're both on the same diet.

Listen up—it's not about the diet. That's the myth we buy into so we can blame the diet. But focusing on the diet is just another way of getting distracted from what it actually *is* about. When we struggle with weight (or money or relationships or alcohol), distraction is very convenient: it keeps us from having to deal with what's really eating us.

Let's talk about Mary, because there's something about Mary that is familiar to anyone who has ever found herself stuck in that mind-mystifying pattern of Cry-Eat-Repeat-WTF?!

- Mary tells herself she's fat and ugly. This is Mary's typical mind-set on any given day.
- This makes Mary feel "disgusting." She's also afraid that she'll be fat and ugly and therefore unlovable forever.
- Mary decides to go on "the banana diet" to lose weight because her friend "lost a ton of weight" eating bananas. Oh, and also because Mary says she loves bananas. Going on a banana diet makes sense, given Mary's mind-set.
- As per the diet's requirements Mary proclaims just about all food off-limits: bread, sugar, salt, pasta, meat, potatoes, dairy, wheat, gluten, alcohol, fried anything, sugar-free anything, everything and anything that Mary loves to eat. The only foods she's "allowed" to eat are bananas, certain vegetables, and chicken, but only at dinnertime. Mary thinks the Banana Diet might be "the answer" she's been seeking for so long. Mary, an otherwise intelligent adult woman, somehow thinks going on this particular diet is a good idea.
- Mary immediately has a heightened awareness of all the foods she's restricted herself from having. She feels "deprived."
- By dinnertime on day two Mary comes unglued. She draws the blinds in her house and tells everyone she's going away for a while because she's afraid of acting like a bona fide head-banging banshee in public. Starvation really doesn't become her, poor thing.
- Mary also has a love-hate relationship with the bathroom scale. It all depends on what it "says" to her each morning (and sometimes again at night) but it's usually something like, "Die, *Bitch*."
- Mary notices her knuckles are as white as snow.
- On day three, Mary cries uncle and goes off the diet.

- She looks in the mirror and calls herself all sorts of nasty names.
- Then she cries.
- Then she eats.
- Then she repeats the process all over again.

Mary feels like a failure.

Is it because the diet didn't work?

No! (Did you say yes?)

It's because Mary buys into the D-Myth: that it's the diet's fault. She's never actually *willing* to work any of the diets she chooses, which is why she goes into resistance mode. Why does she keep doing this? Because she is *out of her mind* when she decides, "it's time to go on a diet." She's neither motivated nor inspired by the diet (despite her love of bananas). In fact, it doesn't matter which diet Mary chooses—it could be the healthiest diet in the world—because her mind is programmed to check out whenever it comes to food and eating and all matters concerning her weight. No matter what she eats or doesn't eat, Mary can't win because she is "unconscious" and unaware of why she does what she does to her body.

So, what exactly was Mary thinking (and feeling) when she decided to go on her banana diet? Recall, she was telling herself that she was fat and ugly. She was *afraid* of her weight. Her motivation to go on a diet was fear. When you allow yourself to be motivated by fear, how long do you suspect the motivation will last? A day? A week? A month or two? It's hard to say exactly—everyone is different—but one thing is for sure: her motivation won't last forever. Using fear as a motivator is exhausting. It's an energy drain and a happiness buster. Mary's Self and her body naturally fight back: her Self sends signals that the banana diet is not dignified (which she ignores) and her body finally rebels (because it's just not into starvation). It's a war that Mary simply cannot win, at least not for long.

Welcome to Mary's diet mentality *hell*, a self-imposed prison from which she has no clue how to escape because she's not even aware she's in it. She is forever caught up in the Cry-Eat-Repeat cycle: She beats herself up. She feels desperate. This makes her **cry**. She decides to **eat** to make herself feel better. This causes her to gain more weight. **Repeat.** In desperation, Mary next tries the "lentils and beans diet" she read about in a magazine, not because she thinks it's healthy but because...

Mary thinks: "I'm afraid I'll be fat forever."

Mary feels: Desperate.

Mary does: Another diet.

But no matter which diet Mary chooses, the outcome is the same (she gives up) because fear is the motivator.

Mary thinks: "I'm afraid I'll be fat forever."

Mary feels: Fear (a.k.a. desperate).

Mary does: "The chicken, rice, and broccoli diet" (because "this time" she's going to "do it right").

As long as she remains unconscious as to why she does what she does, Mary will continue the pattern and the result will always be the same, no matter what the diet. Such is the power of the D-Myth—it sets you up to fall back down.

Whenever you're locked in a fear-based mind-set regarding your weight, the last thing you need to do is go on a diet, *any* diet, because that will just fuel your fear of being deprived. And you will use that as proof that "diets don't work."

When you go on a diet using fear as a motivator you'll have to rely on willpower to carry you through. And we all know how that ends.

Anytime we do anything in an "unconscious" state of mind we set ourselves up to fail and delude ourselves further by believing "the diet didn't work." The truth is—and I realize it's harsh—you had no Dignity when you went on the diet. The diet didn't fail you. *You* failed you. You failed to take care of your Self, first. Sorry, Mama Bear.

But guess what? Failure is an AFGO—another opportunity to get conscious. In fact, failure is a gift because it offers you a chance to start paying attention to what you're really hungry for.

## YOU, YOUR SELF, AND YOUR MIND

The Dignity Diet is grounded in conscious awareness of how you're feeling and then re-calibrating your mind so that your feelings don't drive you to take actions that are undignified. Instead of fear it uses love as a motivating force.

In order to stay conscious try this: whenever you're about to eat something, ask yourself, "Does eating this dignify my deepest desires?"

Then, decide. Make a conscious choice to eat it or not eat it. It's entirely your choice, and believing otherwise is a lie that keeps you in the struggle.

Believing that you don't have time to prepare your lunch…

Believing that you had to eat the donuts because that's all that was available at the time…

Believing you couldn't resist the food at the party because you have no control when it comes to food…

*maybe it's not true*

Believing you were too busy at work to because you had to meet a deadline…

These are all lovely excuses we tell ourselves when we are unconscious and they are founded in the underlying belief that we are victims of our circumstances—that we "have to" do certain things; that we "should choose this and not that"; and that we "have no choice" but to follow "the rules."

Not true. Not true. Not true.

Life is full of rules. Even diets have "rules." And you don't have to follow any of them if you don't want to. In fact, there is nothing in this life that you have to do. This is another one of those things that is worth repeating because we tend to not really hear it:

*There is nothing in this life
that you have to do.*

And if you don't believe that, you cannot be free.

You will never feel like you are in control of your life.

But when, on the other hand, you look at everything you do as a choice you make, you will feel empowered. Even when the choice is to eat the donut. The key is to stay conscious and aware of the choices you make every day. All day long. Own your decisions. Stop making excuses. Own your choices. And don't be surprised by the outcomes they create—own those too.

To wit:

"I choose not to prepare lunch for myself because I believe I don't have time. Later, when I stop for fast food, I won't pretend to not understand why it happened."

"I choose to eat this donut and I will not blame the scale if my weight goes up."

"I choose to eat this party food—the food can't make me do it. I am making me do it."

"I choose to make my work more important than feeding my body in a dignified way and I now see that's why my body is overweight."

When you take responsibility for every choice you make, you step into your power. You take responsibility for your life. You are an Adult.

Believing we don't have a choice is very fattening.

**New Rule: Only you have the power to make and break all the rules.**

The choice is always yours.

## THE HOPE DIET

Even the healthiest, cleanest, doctor-recommended diet is going to have rules telling you to eat this, not that. But if you're not ready to go "all in" with a particular diet and the rules it espouses, *but you do it anyway*, you're on what I call the Hope Diet: you hope that a miracle will occur and you will somehow find a way to white-knuckle through it, and that all the weight will come off once and for all.

The Hope Diet is hope*less* because it takes your Self out of the equation; it puts you at the mercy of an external force that you hope will fix you. The truth is, going on a Hope Diet, whether it's Weight Watchers, or Paleo, or even the banana diet, can't work unless you're *all in*; unless you consciously choose to follow the diet because it feels like love—it truly feels like you are taking care of your body. If there is any doubt in your mind about whether the diet is right for you or good for you or exciting enough for you, then you're on another version of the Hope Diet—you're just keeping your fingers crossed behind your own back, hoping it'll work.

## CHILD MIND VS. ADULT MIND

Think of it this way, you have one brain and *three* minds: there's your Child Mind, your Adult Mind, and then there's your true Self, the part of you that *knows* without thinking.

Your Child Mind is emotionally immature—it struggles in its ability to handle emotions such as anger, fear, jealousy, and disappointment. Your Child Mind learned its emotional responses before your brain was fully developed, which didn't occur until somewhere around the age of twenty-five. Nevertheless,

Child Mind and its limited ability to use logic and reason often stays in control of our lives well into our twenties and beyond. The problem is, it doesn't have a clue how to use the full deck it now has to play with.

In other words, your life, or at least the parts that feel out of control, are being run by your Child Mind using a less-than-full deck of cards. She means well, but she doesn't have any idea how to run an adult life.

Adult Mind comes with age *and* practice, but only if we call it into action, and that's often a pretty big "if." Adult Mind is capable of responsible decision-making and high-level reasoning skills. It also has the ability to delay gratification for the greater good of your Self. These are all signs of an emotionally mature *adult* mind-set.

Your true Self is the part of you that observes all the thoughts your mind thinks, both from a Child and Adult Mind perspective. Your true Self is connected to your body and your soul and the entire Universe and, therefore, has a much bigger perspective of your whole life and how you fit in it. Your Self is the unchanged part of the person you were on the day you were born. It has never lost sight of your Dignity. It always knows what's best for you.

If you want to know what you really *want*, ask your Self. Your Adult Mind has the ability to access the deepest parts of your Self, which has nothing but love for the part of you that still thinks like a child. After all, your Child Mind cannot see what it's incapable of seeing—that's a job for Adult Mind. If you want to think like an adult you must consciously step into your Adult Mind and question what your Child Mind keeps telling you, such as:

- You *have to* follow the diet. (I do?)
- You *shouldn't* eat that. (Says who?)

- That food is *forbidden*. (According to whose rules?)
- You're going to get in *trouble*. (Really? My knees are shaking.)
- That's not what you're *supposed* to do. (Sue me!)
- You've been such a *bad girl*. (Sticks and stones.)
- This cookie is a reward for being such a *good girl*. (Oh, honey, I love you. But we don't need rewards like this.)

It's hard to hear your Child Mind think when you're eyeball deep in its thoughts. You must first step out of Child Mind, and that's not easy to do unless you first get conscious of the thoughts it's thinking. Then you can step into Adult Mind and challenge those thoughts, like we did above.

As far as it's concerned, Child Mind is the boss, and it has no intention of stepping down from its perch: it'll take conscious effort on your part to make Adult Mind your default thinker. Child Mind is what keeps you locked in stage 1. Adult Mind is what can set you free.

Surely you've already met your Adult Mind. Think of a time when you typically feel in charge, in control, and at peace. Perhaps it's when you're at work or when you're in parenting mode or when you're in charge of planning a major fundraising event. *That* is the mind-set you're after: in charge, in control, and at peace. That's the way you want to feel when you're "on" a diet. That's how you know you're honoring your Self.

## WILLPOWER VS. WILLINGNESS POWER

There are two power sources that make a diet work. The first one hurts, from a little to a lot. The second one doesn't hurt at all.

## POWER SOURCE #1: WILLPOWER

Willpower is the use of mental force to induce action, no matter what emotion we may be experiencing. No motivation? Call on willpower to push you through. Willpower, however, is an unsustainable energy resource. It requires that you force a diet to work for you, no matter how much you may be resisting the diet. We resort to willpower when we're actually *un*willing to take action.

## POWER SOURCE #2: WILLINGNESS POWER

Willingness power, on the other hand, is effortless because it is channeled from your deepest desires. It is sustainable because it feeds on itself. Unlike willpower, it doesn't burn out unless you allow it to burn out. Willingness power springs forth from the desire to pay attention to your Self. When your mind-set is powered by willingness, you have an endless supply of mental energy to work the diet. In fact, you might even be excited to be on the diet, no matter which diet you've chosen. Willingness power blows our mind wide open

Remember, it's not about whether diets work; it's about how you work (or don't work) the diet.

# RESPONSIBILITY: STEPPING INTO YOUR ADULT SHOES

Stage 2 is about taking responsibility. Are you willing to take full responsibility for reclaiming your Dignity? Are you willing to take full responsibility for how much your body weighs today? If not, stop right here. This journey cannot begin unless and until you are willing to take full responsibility for the body you have, and the body you are about to create. All of your choices, conscious or otherwise, have created the body you have. And all of your choices going forward are entirely up to you.

It's tempting to come up with all sorts of reasons and excuses for why things haven't worked in the past and why they may not work going forward, but that is not helpful here. You are in charge. This is your body to heal. When you take responsibility, you no longer sit back and blame the diet or anything else for "making" you feel any one or all of the following:

- Hungry
- Restricted
- Miserable
- Disgusted
- Horrible
- Lonely
- Sad
- Deprived
- Seriously pissed off!

No one and no thing can ever *make* you feel any of those emotions. If you feel a negative emotion when you're on a diet, it's because of the way you're thinking: your mind-set is causing you to resist, and whenever you're feeling resistance, you're not being responsible to your body. You're not listening to your Self.

When we don't take responsibility we become helpless victims; we blame some outside force that is inexplicably working against us. We live in the land of make believe, where believing we're powerless allows us to abdicate the responsibility we have to create a meaningful and purposeful life.

like what children do. When we're stuck in a child's mind-set of looking to people, places, and things to "make us happy," we pay little attention to the choices we make. We often think we have no choice.

As an adult you always have a choice. Have I beaten that drum loudly enough yet?

Taking responsibility creates room for willingness to emerge. Going on a diet when you are not willing is like making a sandwich without bothering to put anything in between the two pieces of bread.

The Dignity Diet would never have you do anything against your will. But even though you may still be in resistance mode in stage 2, you may be starting to sense that it's loosening its grip. Remember, this is no time to go on any kind of diet. Besides, you cannot know which diet is best for you until you get your Dignity back.

This is a stage of contemplation and introspection. We're throwing out the old maps and charting a new course for your weight loss journey. We're asking questions that will give us some insight into why things haven't worked in the past.

If any of the previous diets you chose to go on in the past "didn't work," it wasn't because of the diets—it was because of your mind-set. This is a very important distinction because it forces you to be accountable to your *Self*, especially if you choose to go on a diet that goes against the will of your body. So it's important to ask:

- Why did I choose to go on that particular diet?
- Why did I choose to go off that diet?
- At any point before starting the diet, was I unwilling?

- If so, what made me think it would be a good idea to go on the diet?
- How was I *feeling* before I started the diet? Why?
- How did I feel on day one of the diet? Why?
- What was I feeling at the moment I decided to go off the diet? Why?

The purpose of these questions is to ascertain your mind-set (What was your experience before, during, and after the diet?), and to get you to accept responsibility for the way you were *thinking* and *feeling* and *doing* the diet because your TFD is what determines the probability of success.

See if any of these thoughts sound familiar:

- I have to lose this weight because I have a high school reunion to go to (which caused you to feel stressed).
- My cholesterol is too high (which caused you to feel scared).
- My friend lost a lot of weight on this diet (which caused you to feel jealous).
- I can't stand the thought of not eating the foods I love (which caused you to feel deprived).
- This is going to be so difficult (which caused you to feel powerless and helpless).

Notice the feeling each of those thoughts creates. Is it any wonder we don't succeed in our weight loss efforts? How can we expect to take inspired action when we're feeling stressed, scared, jealous, deprived, or hopeless and helpless?

Each of those thoughts above is an example of how we abdicate responsibility for the feelings we create and the actions we take in your power to choose, you will make undignified choices. Whatever you decide to do, it is your decision to make.

Just remember: whenever your actions come from a place of love and inspiration, you will experience joy. It's all about you. It's all *on* you. It's your life. If you choose to accept this, *live* it like you mean it, and take responsibility for the outcomes you create by first taking responsibility for the thoughts you think, the feelings you feel, and the actions you take as a result. Then, don't be surprised by the outcome. It's usually pretty predictable.

Going on a diet *unwillingly* and without eagerness is disrespectful to your Self. It is rather undignified to treat your Self that way, don't you think?

Are you ready to go on a Heroine's Journey? Would you be willing to slay dragons in order to treat yourself with loving kindness? Do you believe you are worth loving? Are you ready to find out more about your Self? What is it that she *really* wants and what keeps her from getting it? Your decision to lose weight (or not) is a decision only you can make. Above all else, protect your right to feel good in your body, and honor your responsibility to make it happen.

But even if you choose not to take responsibility, notice that, and ask yourself why. Perhaps the first leg of your journey is to find out what's causing the resistance. Remember, Self respect requires that you do *nothing* against your will.

Take a moment to think about what you're willing to do starting right now. Don't worry; it can be the tiniest of steps. If it moves you forward even a millimeter, then you will have started your Heroine's Journey.

Right now I am willing to _____

because _____

If it feels like love you're ready to move on.

# THE DIGNITY DIET: TRY A LITTLE R.E.S.P.E.C.T.

Dignity is the ultimate source of inspiration behind your willing-ness power as well as your ability to take responsibility for your own happiness in life.

Dignity springs from love of your Self. And your body. But if you're still finding it hard to love your body, try a little respect. It deserves at least that much, don't you think? After all, where would you be without it?

Think about it: Your body has been a slave to your whims and wishes for many years. Even when it's not in perfect health, it keeps on keepin' on, for *you*. Your heart keeps pumping, your lungs keep expanding and contracting, your insides do their best to keep you alive and kicking.

Imagine what your body could do if it were treated with kindness and respect and the Dignity it deserves. Think about how you feel when someone disrespects you. Why would it be OK for you to disrespect your Self?

If you say you want to lose weight, perhaps it's time to get on the same side as your body, especially since it's always been there for you.

When you have Dignity, you choose to feed your body well, and you trust it to tell you when to eat and how much.

## READY TO MOVE ON TO STAGE 3?

Use the following checklist to determine whether you're ready for stage 3. Unless you can check them all, go back and review stage 2 before moving ahead.

☐ You are willing to look at the word "diet" in a whole new way.

☐ You're ready to step into your *adult* Self and take responsibility for your weight, your body, and your health, because…

☐ Taking responsibility doesn't scare you (much).

☐ You're starting to really fall in love… with your Self.

☐ You. Are. Willing. To. Move. *Forward.*

# STAGE 3

# Taking the Training Wheels Off A.K.A. "Kiss My Fat Ass, Baby"

## THE SIZE OF YOUR ASS IS NOBODY'S BUSINESS BUT YOURS

Do you recall when a tabloid magazine published photos of former Victoria's Secret supermodel, Tyra Banks, in a bathing suit, under headlines that read "TYRA PORKCHOPS" and "AMERICA'S NEXT TOP WADDLE"? Did Tyra crumble? Did she curl up into a fetal position, or worse, starve herself into conformity? No. Instead she fired off a salvo that went something like this: *Kiss my fat ass...A woman's worth does not depend on what anyone else thinks about her ass.*

Now *that's* how you come out with all buns blazing and your Dignity fully intact. Even if it did sting to be called names on the front pages of sleazy tabloids, Tyra's message was loud, clear, and dignified: my ass is *my* business.

That girl is fearless.

# FEAR IS FATTENING

Fear's a bitch. And it's full of fat. But get this: where there is Dignity, there can be no fear (unless, of course, you're being chased by an axe-wielding maniac dressed in a clown suit, then you ought to run like the dickens).

The kind of fear we conjure up in our minds produces a bottom-less pit of emotional hunger. It's a sort of synthetic fear—it's not real, but it can sure feel like it is. One of the biggest things we fear is what other people think. It can drive us mad—it can drive us straight to food. How many times have you heard yourself say, "I don't care what other people think," as you wolf down a cheese-burger, fries, and a diet soda spiked with your mascara-filled tears?

It's one thing to *say* you don't care and quite another to really *feel* the freedom that comes with not giving a damn what other people think; in other words, to truly be fearless.

# FAT IS NOT THE ENEMY

Fat is just a word. It's not even a four-letter word, yet it gets treated as such. The dictionary meaning of the word "fat," as it pertains to the human body, is an excess amount of flesh. Notice it does not say an excess and *ugly* amount of flesh; nor does it say an excess and *disgusting* amount of flesh. The more adjectives we use to describe "fat," the more fattening it becomes. The more we think of fat as the enemy, the fatter we tend to become.

If you have an excess amount of flesh on your body in the form of fat, that's *your* business. What other people have to say about your fat reveals more about them than it does about you. And what you have to say about your fat tells you a lot about you, too, because the less you think of your Self, the less dignified you will be, and the fatter you will get.

Carla (whose back-side was bigger than she wanted it to be) used to cringe at the word "fat." She preferred to use a ten-letter word to describe the size of her butt: "overweight." Carla told me that her biggest fear was being called a "fat bitch." It didn't take long for Carl's fear to rear its ugly head as we talked. She told me that every time she went anywhere, she worried that someone would call her out for being a fat bitch.

I asked Carla which word bothered her more—being called fat or being called a bitch. Without hesitating she said fat. She could think of no greater insult than being called fat.

As a result, Carla, who was by all accounts was carrying about forty extra pounds, would hide her body in baggy clothes. She was hoping and praying she could successfully pull a fast one on everyone.

Carla told me that just hearing the word "fat" caused a visceral reaction that would suddenly make her feel nauseous, especially when it was used to describe *someone who was actually fat*.

I asked Carla if *she* thought she was fat.

Silence.

"OK, let me ask you this: Are you a bitch?"

"Yeah, sometimes, I'm sure I am. I can be bitchy, but that's not who I *am*," she answered without hesitation. Clearly the B word wasn't an issue at all.

Not one to leave a stone unturned, I asked another question.

seemed to be able to do it. And she couldn't figure out why. She'd never realized that her fear was so damn fattening because it made her want to eat more.

So, instead of going on a calorie-restricted diet, I suggested Carla go on a fear-restricted diet that went like this: instead of trying to count calories or fat grams or sugar grams, I suggested she count the number of times she felt fear or its cousins, worry, anxiety, distrust, disrespect, and shame, throughout her day. Since awareness is the first step toward conquering fear (and fat), I advised Carla to check in with her Self throughout the day, preferably every hour, and to e-mail me at the end of the day with her results.

At the end of the first day, Carla was shocked by the number of times she had felt a fear-based feeling throughout the day.

She was afraid to eat breakfast because it would make her fat.

She felt extremely anxious when the office manager brought donuts for everyone and put them in the staff kitchen for all to enjoy.

She felt uptight when her boss called her into his office.

She was worried about getting her work done in time for the deadline.

She worried about what to make for dinner.

She was afraid she wouldn't have time to make dinner and that she'd pig out on junk food instead.

Eventually, Carla was able to connect the dots between thinking a negative fear-based *thought,* how that thought made her *feel* (afraid, worried, etc.), and how that feeling determined what she would *do* next (eat or not eat).

Fear has the power to make you fat.

It can turn you into an alcoholic.

It can make you turn to drugs.

It can make you go broke.

In short, fear can make us do some crazy stuff, not because we are actually crazy, but because we know no other way to stop the craziness in our heads.

And the craziest thing of all is that we don't even realize we're feeling it. Fear can become such a conditioned response that it feels *normal*. In fact, most people don't even think to call it fear.

But it's precisely that desperation to *not* feel a feeling that makes us head straight for the cupcake or the Doritos or the M&M's.

In effect, we give food the responsibility for making us feel better.

So, let's do the math:

Fear of Fat + Fear of Feeling a Feeling =
*HOLY BLOODY HELL, I CAN'T BELIEVE I ATE THE WHOLE THING!*

Think about it: if you're afraid of being fat or getting fat *and* you're triggered into feeling a feeling you don't like feeling, what are you likely going to *do*?

Eat or not eat?

Drink or not drink?

Shop or not shop?

When your mind has you backed into a corner, the only thing you want to do is run away. It's what you've been *conditioned* to do.

And it makes damn good sense. Neuroscience has shown that our patterned Think-Feel-Do responses to the people, places, and things in our lives actually become hardwired in our brains.

Very hard. And very wired.

*Think* a thought.

*Feel* a feeling.

*Do* that-thing-you-do.

For example:

> Think: "I hate my job."

> Feel: Frustrated.

> Do: Eat cake.

Thinking the thought, "I hate my job," is an utterly useless thought, unless it motivates you to make a change. Unless you can find a way to make it useful, ditch the thought. In other words, if you can't make the thought work for you instead of against you, ditch it.

Here's the only way it can work for you:

Think: "I hate my job."

Feel: Motivated.

Do: Find another job.

The difference between the two TFD models above is that, in the first one, the belief is, "I hate my job <u>and</u> I'm stuck here." In the second one, the belief is, "I hate my job <u>and</u> I have the power to do something about it."

Big difference.

If you really want to stop eating cake, you're going to have to step into your power.

Change your TFD.

Take responsibility.

Stop finding excuses to eat cake.

❮❯

The point here is not to get you to instantly feel happy and excited; the point is to get you to see how you create so much extra (and prolonged) pain for yourself by adding on layers of painful (fearful) thinking that keeps you frozen in time.

Believing that you are destined to remain stuck anywhere is poisonous to your mental health.

When we decide to choose what we want to believe, we also choose how we want to feel. Why would you ever want to choose frustration?

The first step toward taking your power back is to become aware of when fear shows up at your doorstep. Pinpoint the thought that creates the feeling of fear (I hate my job). Then find the underlying belief (*and* I'm stuck here). Then notice what that feeling makes you want to *do* (eat cake).

## HOW TO MAKE FEAR PLAY BY THE RULES

You know fear is going to come to visit. Be prepared. Here's what to do when it shows up.

1. Tell your fear it must knock first. This requires you to *listen* for the knock; otherwise, it will just let itself in and follow you everywhere. The knock is the *feeling*. What does Fear feel like to you?

2. Tell fear it must sit in the corner. This will shrink it down to size. Since I'm such a visual person, it helps me to literally tell fear where it is allowed to sit—usually in a chair in the corner somewhere where I can keep a constant (mindful) eye on it.

3. Be vigilant. Make sure fear stays in the corner. Talk to it: "Yo! Hey. Yeah, you. Sit your ass back down in that corner. And while you're at it, put a sock in it. Can't you see I'm practicing the violin?"

4. When (if) you are able to put enough space between you and fear, then and only then can you allow it to speak. Ask it where it came from and why it's been following you around. What is fear trying to teach you about your Self?

The point isn't to eradicate fear but to stop running from it. This is how we manage our emotions. After all, fear can't chase you if you stop running. When we learn to manage our mind and the feelings it creates, we are no longer running. We realize we have choices in what we think and therefore how we feel. When we take back control of our mind, fear puts its pouty self in the corner. And then it leaves. It can't stand to be ignored.

When our actions aren't being driven by fear, we make room for our Self to appear. Your Self does a much better job of using *free will* to skip the cake and cookies and make choices that serve your best interests. And sometimes, by gosh by golly, your Self may choose to eat the cake and cookies *and* enjoy them thoroughly. Guilt, another one of fear's cousins, also learns to stay in the corner.

## WORRY

Worry is fear's first cousin. The biggest misconception so many of us have about worry is that by focusing on that which makes us afraid, we think we can somehow avert a crisis. We think worry is the price we have to pay to keep the worst things from happening to us. We believe that if we don't worry, the Universe will catch us by surprise and say, "Gotcha!"

We're not necessarily consciously aware of this. Since worry becomes something many of us can do on autopilot (i.e., without conscious awareness), we become used to worry. Sometimes we even get comfortable with it because we believe it's necessary and normal.

For example, I learned to worry at a very young age, so that by the time I became a mother, I was a full-fledged expert at worrying. Expert, I tell you! I could create the most upsetting, terrifying circumstances in my mind, most of which involved an incurable disease, much pain and suffering, and an untimely death. Fear chased me everywhere, no matter how fast I ran.

And then one day I stopped running and got curious. I wanted to look behind me to see what the hell I was running from. Where did this ever present worry come from, and who invited it here? (Hi, Mom!) Why was I always going down the road of "what if"?

Consciously watching your mind conjure up worry is a fascinating experiment in both logic and nonsense. It's a real trip and one so worth taking.

One of the best ways I learned to thwart my worrying mind was to consult with my Self, who happens to be the smartest person I know when it comes to understanding me. Accessing my Self wasn't always easy, however, because my mind wanted to stay in charge. Talking to my Self required that I transcend my mind. (Insert music from the old Twilight television series here.)

This is when curiosity becomes your new best friend. Curiosity is so much better than cake, and it can have long-lasting (positive) results.

There is an almost instant shift in mood (even if ever so slight) that occurs when we merely question the fearful thoughts that lead to worry. It's not that we attempt to take a quantum leap from believing to disbelieving (Because quantum leaps aren't possible, remember?), but rather that we go from believing to questioning. It's a slight but powerful shift in taking back control from your mind.

But who, or what, are we questioning exactly? If we question the mind it will just spit back the worrisome thought (I think I might have a disease), or, it will cleverly give us a logical reason why it's silly to think that way, as if it weren't responsible for its own thinking! Don't fall for that last one. That's your mind's version of a head fake. It knows the "right" answer and it will serve it up to you on a platter because it doesn't want you to dig deeper. This is why relying on logic isn't going to be helpful.

Dig deeper. Don't be afraid to piss off your mind.

Talk to your Self.

When I first started talking to my Self in this way it felt like I was in an arm wrestle with my mind, which seemed to get severely pissed off at my attempts to bypass it. My mind wanted to hold onto its position of authority. It didn't want to hear me talking to my Self. It didn't like being ignored.

Since I had learned not to let my mind scare me so easily, I persisted. I asked my all-knowing Self the following question from a place of genuine curiosity: "What if something bad does happen?" And, "Do I actually believe I can stop it from happening by worrying?"

And then right on cue, and before my Self could answer in a kind and compassionate way, my mind rudely interrupted with, *Pfffft, of course not. Don't be ridiculous.*

Mayday! Mayday! *Head fake.* I could see it, so I persisted in try-ing to have a conversation with my Self, rather than with my mas-sively condescending mind.

*Dear Self, WTF is going on? Why do I keep thinking such painfully worrisome thoughts? Do I actually believe worrying is going to help?*

And then I waited for a reply. It took a while because my interrupting mind kept trying to weasel its way back in: *Just be logical, that's all. There's nothing to actually worry about. Look around, everything's fine. And, by the way, did you hear that it's going to be the worst hurricane season on record and...*

Shut the Fritos up!

(Sigh. If only yelling at the mind were enough. If so, I would've stopped worrying a long time ago.)

If we don't spot the head fake, we take our mind at face value, and that can be very dangerous.

There is a part of each of us that is smarter than our own mind, and when we learn how to turn down the incessant chatter we make room for the Self to speak. This was my Self's message to me:

Dear Beautiful One,

You are afraid that you cannot handle your own fear. You believe that you cannot endure whatever life has in store for you. Whatever it is, remember that You chose this life for all that it would teach you about You. Everything that has happened and everything that will happen must be exactly that way in order to learn the lessons you seek. Wondering or worrying about the future will not stop anything from happening.

And that is OK. You will be OK. And this is why:

72

The Universe trusted You when You said You wanted this life. You also trusted the Universe to give You the life You needed to live and learn and grow. Everything always turns out exactly the way it's supposed to. Fear has neither the business nor the power to change that.

Focus, instead, on love. And gratitude. And grace. Those things will see You through. Therefore, I say to you, let go.

Let it all go. Learn to trust the power of You.

With massive amounts of love, trust, and gratitude for how hard you're rocking the shiitakes out of this life,

Your Self

Well, when you put it *that* way...

It was enough to make a grown-up girl cry.

It turns out I was so much smarter than I had given my Self credit for.


## BETTER-FEELING THOUGHTS: YOUR MIND'S VERSION OF A HEAD FAKE

There are two ways to approach changing the mind: linearly and vertically. Linear thought work is useful, but temporary—it's basically a *head fake* designed to make us think, "Eureka, I have fixed myself once and for all." When our thought work is linear, we often fall for the so-called "better-feeling" thought—the head fake. Linear thought work brings temporary relief because it keeps us on the surface of our mind, at thought level.

It looks like this:

**Old (lousy feeling) irrational thought:** "My child is sick and I'm afraid she has an incurable disease and she will die."

**New (better-feeling) rational thought:** "She's just got a cold, for heaven's sake. I'm being ridiculous."

The second thought actually does feel better, but the relief is often temporary. That's because better-feeling thoughts, while they bring relief in the moment, occur at thought level and can only be as good as the underlying beliefs that support them. If we don't address the underlying beliefs ("The world is a scary place and I'm going to be punished by having everything good in my life taken away from me."), the mind will eventually serve up another familiar and painful thought. When our mind is in the habit of going to the worst-case scenario, logic isn't going to change those thought habits; the underlying fears must be addressed in order to create a lasting shift.

## LINEAR THOUGHT WORK: SHORT-TERM RELIEF

By now you've notice how predictable the mind can be; it offers up the same old thought patterns again and again. If it starts to feel like we're going in circles, that's because we are, which is why we keep shaking our heads: we thought we had dealt with this already, *dammit*!

But thought work must, at some point, become vertical in order to have a lasting effect: we must be willing to look deep down into the unconscious mind where our beliefs are tucked away. We have to go digging beyond the mind's pat answers to uncover the beliefs that create our day-to-day fearful thoughts and thought patterns, because the thoughts on the surface (the ones we're aware of) are driven by the programming that's deep below thought level.

## VERTICAL THOUGHT WORK: LONG-LASTING RELIEF

### Thought Level
**Painful Thought You're Currently Thinking**

⬇

### Unconscious Mind
**Belief System That Drives The Way You Think**

⬇

### Dis-Belief
**Challenging/Dismantling Painful Beliefs**

The deeper answers have the potential to create profound energetic or vibrational shifts that are *experiential*. The more fear you release, the higher your vibrational frequency. It's as if the deeper we go, the less we think and the more we experience a shift in being. The more we can get out of the mind, the more we can connect to our higher Self. Our Self can teach us about our strength and our resilience. Our Self never lost its Dignity.

Thinking is overrated. This is why we must be wary of those better-feeling thoughts. They may make a lot of sense, but that's not how to judge their value. Thoughts that become beliefs that create lasting peace of mind are the most valuable of all. Those kinds of thoughts, which come from realizations, have the power to change your attitude, your overall outlook on life, and general sense of well-being in profound ways. It's experiential: you feel the relief in your heart, not your head.

And for anyone who says, "Easier said than done," I offer you a well-intentioned kick in the ass: This is not meant to be easy or hard. It just is what it is. The only way through is *through*. Attempting to go around is why you keep coming around full circle to where you are now: stuck. Again.

Remember, quantum leaping is for subatomic particles, which, alas, you are not. Humans must settle for passing through each of the points that exist between A and B. If A equals the belief that worrying helps keep disaster at bay, and B equals the realization that worry serves no purpose whatsoever, how long it takes you to move through the points in between is entirely up to you. There is no magic formula or specified amount of time. It all depends on how deeply you hold a belief to be true and your willingness to test its veracity.

Since a belief is not a fact, any and all bad-feeling beliefs can be dispelled where there is a desire to feel better. Unlike facts, beliefs are not provable, and that means they are optional and changeable.

So how do you know when to dispel a belief and when to keep it? By the way it makes you *feel*. If your priority is to feel peace, joy, gratitude, connected, or any other variation of happiness, then your beliefs must be aligned with the desire to feel the way you want to feel. Fear-based beliefs will not serve you; on the contrary, they'll only make you miserable.

**Uncovering a fear-based thought as well as the underlying thoughts and beliefs that support it is how we go "vertical" in our thought work.**

## SHAME

Alexis always struggled with her weight, even though by most accounts she was not overweight. Many would describe Alexis's weight as "normal," perhaps not by Hollywood standards, but certainly by real-world standards.

Alexis vigilantly kept track of her weight and stepped on the scale as many as half a dozen times a day. When I asked her why she weighed herself so often, she said it was because she was afraid of gaining weight.

Hmmmm. Sound rational? Let's continue.

I then asked Alexis how weighing herself kept her from gaining weight. She said that when the number went up, which it invariably did after she had something to eat or drink, she would stop eating. When I asked her how she decided when to start eating again, she said she would wait for as long as she could—which usually meant starvation—then she would eat again, weigh herself, freak out, then starve herself all over again.

"So, Alexis, you realize that a big glass of water, while calorie- and fat-free, will cause the number on the scale to go up, right?" I asked her.

"Um…maybe, but that doesn't matter. It still freaks me out."

"Why?"

"Because. It just does."

"Why?"

"I don't know. It just does. It always has."

"Yes, I understand that, but it would be really good to know why. What does it mean if the number goes up a pound or two?"

"It means I ate too much."

"But what if it's mostly water? Do you take that into consideration, at least?"

"No."

"Why not?"

"Because it doesn't matter—if the number on the scale goes up, no matter what the reason, then I freak out. I stop eating. I won't even drink any water."

"For how long?"

"For as long as I can stand it. I used to be able to go a whole day without eating, but I can't do that anymore. These days the most I can go without eating is about eight hours. Then I cave."

I should mention that Alexis is a forty-one-year-old woman, a mother of three, and a senior executive for a major retailer. When she's in "work mode" she thrives: she feels in charge and in control. She's a major asset to the company she works for, and she demands a salary that is commensurate with her talents.

And yet, outside of her career she feels the opposite: out of control, undervalued, and unappreciated. Food brings her brief moments of solace and extended bouts of anxiety.

Alexis's fear of becoming overweight was all-consuming. When she first hired me, she was extremely reluctant to give up this fear. She believed it was the only thing motivating her to keep her weight "under control." Despite her confidence in her ability to drive her company's profits up, she had no confidence whatsoever in her ability to keep her weight down without fear as a motivator. Alexis was smart enough to see how illogical her thoughts were, but that didn't matter. Fear had her in its grip, and it wasn't about to let go easily. For Alexis, going from point A (I must keep my weight under control.) to point B (I will eat when I'm hungry and stop when my body tells me it has had enough.) was a huge leap. We spent a lot of time working through her long-held belief that following the natural hunger rhythms of her body would be catastrophic. As we went vertical, Alexis discovered fear's best friend: shame.

Alexis's shame went deep, which is why it was such a surprise to her when she uncovered it. How could a high-powered and successful woman like her ever feel such a "lowly" feeling as shame? She thought it was beneath her. But there it was. Where did it come from? And how had it stayed so well hidden for so many years? Alexis said she never would've suspected she had shame. She worked hard to exude confidence.

And that's why so many of us get lured into the "I need to feel self-confident" trap. It's a way to cover up shame. But shame continues to work quietly and invisibly in the background, upholding the beliefs that we inherited so long ago. Shame, you see, is the opposite of Dignity. It holds us down instead of lifting us up.

Challenging her beliefs seemed almost sacrilegious, but Alexis trusted that there had to be another way, even though she had yet to figure one out. Her willingness to get curious and go vertical ultimately led Alexis to her Self and a more peaceful way of being in the world. It wasn't until she confronted her deep-seated beliefs around her body and her weight that she realized just how much energy she was spending trying to fight against shame.

## FOOD IS NOT FATTENING

Do you think of food as a friend? Do you turn to food for comfort? Does it make you feel better? Does it talk to you? Does it call your name?

Or perhaps you think of food as your enemy—the cause of your Big Fat Problem and therefore something to be conquered.

Or maybe you have staring contests with food to see who will blink first.

Here's the problem with thinking about food this way:

- Food doesn't have arms. It cannot hug you.
- Food doesn't have a mouth. It cannot call your name.
- Food doesn't have eyes. It cannot stare back at you.

In short: food cannot be your "friend."

Food is just a bunch of ingredients in a bowl.

Some people actually get mad at me when I say that. For them it's tantamount to saying that music is a bunch of notes.

But that's exactly what music is.

Just like a painting is a bunch of brush strokes on a canvas.

And a story is a bunch of words made into sentences and paragraphs and chapters with a beginning, a middle, and an end.

This is an important distinction, but only if your story about food is hurting you. If you weren't an emotional eater struggling with her weight, then it wouldn't matter how you thought about food. I make this distinction only for those who associate food and eating with emotions like comfort, safety, and relief, for example, or anger, loneliness, and boredom, to name a few more. Each of these emotions is generated by the stories we tell ourselves about food.

The question to ask is: Does the story you tell yourself about food *serve* you? Does it result in your having a healthy body or an unhealthy one? Chances are if you're someone who uses food to cover up or stifle painful emotions, your story needs a rewrite.

For example, if you tend to assign food powers it doesn't have, you will find ways to justify eating more food than your body needs. "The food made me do it!" The more you cling to your food stories, the harder it will be to let go of the weight.

- I deserve it. (Don't you deserve good health more?)
- This is my reward. (Why do you need a reward?)
- I've been so good. (Who said you were ever bad?)
- It's not fair. (Who says everything must be fair?)
- It's calling my name. (No, it's not.)
- I'm powerless around food. (Only if you believe it.)
- I can't control myself. (Really?)
- This is my treat. (Is there no better way to treat yourself?)
- I don't want to waste it. (Eating it if you're not hungry is wasteful.)
- It makes me feel better. (How you choose to think about it makes you feel better.)
- What if I can't get enough? (How much is enough?)
- I shouldn't have to deprive myself. (What exactly are you depriving yourself of?)
- If she can eat it, why can't I? (Why does your mind want to go there? How does thinking this way serve you?)
- I can't help it. (Yes you can.)

As you challenge your justifications, notice how old you feel when you're thinking any of the above: Is this a very old and familiar way to think? Do you feel more like a child than an adult? Thoughts like "Food is my reward" and "This is my treat" are things children typically say, and we often carry our childhood mind-set into adulthood. This is why food can be an invitation to grow up, to grow into your Self.

Of course, food can most certainly be a work of art, a masterpiece even; it can create a truly wonderful culinary experience that dazzles the senses. But even though food can be pretty to look at, appreciated, enjoyed, and eaten, it need not be an excuse to abuse our bodies.

When we look to food as a source of comfort or give it qualities only a human friend can have, then we're telling ourselves stories that keep us stuck.

Stripping food down to a bunch of ingredients is one way we can begin to reclaim our power over it. Yes, the ingredients can create something delicious, but that doesn't mean they have to be consumed in quantities beyond that which the human body requires. Food can be enjoyed and appreciated without scarfing down every last morsel out of fear that it will never come around again.

**ᗡᗡ**

Patricia, a client, told me that every time she was invited out to dinner or to any kind of social function at which food would be served, she would worry for days in advance.

What kind of food would be served?

Would she be able to control herself?

She loved hors d'oeuvres and could "never resist them."

Maybe she just wouldn't eat.

But it would take so much effort to not eat.

Screw it. Maybe she shouldn't go; it would be so much easier to just stay home.

These were the thoughts that swirled around in Patricia's mind before going out with her husband and friends; never did she consider who would be there and the good time she might have socializing with her friends. The only thing she could think about was the food.

I asked Patricia what she imagined the evening would be like if she focused on talking to people rather than eating food. She said that was an approach she hadn't thought of even though it sounded so logical.

What was the real purpose of going to the party? If it actually was the food, then why not just eat and run? "That would be rude." OK, then why not just stay home and eat? After all, it wasn't as though Patricia couldn't make delicious little hors d'oeuvres for herself whenever she wanted—she didn't need a party for that. Would it also be considered "rude" to not go to the party?

Do you think that's a stupid question?

The mind spin is never ending. Your mind is a master at putting up roadblocks, and unless you take back the reins, it will block every possible solution with pat answers like "that's rude," "that's not realistic," "that's ridiculous," "that's not fair," "that's not an option," "that's silly," and "that's just plain old stupid."

In other words, the mind will always fight to maintain the status quo. Your job, on the other hand, is to use the thinking (adult) part of your brain to *think* your way out of the status quo, because it's the status quo mind-set that got you where you are today, and you can be sure the status quo mind-set will not get you out.

If you think of food as more than just a bunch of ingredients in a bowl—if, instead, food has become a primary source of pleasure in your life—then we need to cut food down to size, because the way you think about food is not helping you. Food, while necessary for your existence, is also being allowed to mess up your mind.

## THE BATHROOM SCALE: MAYDAY! MAYDAY!

Just as food is merely a bunch of ingredients in a bowl, the bathroom scale is just a heap o' glass, metal, and plastic parts, all meant to provide you with information regarding the weight of your body at any given point in time. The scale spits out data, not opinion. It gives you the facts, just the facts.

Nothing actually happens to you when you step on the scale. You don't suddenly become fat. You are the exact same person and the exact same weight before, during, and after stepping on the scale. Nothing in your world changes in the moment it takes you to weigh your body—mere seconds have passed between stepping on and stepping off.

And yet, what a difference a few seconds can make! Depending on what the scale "says," you will either have a good day or another one of those very bad, terrible, awful days. Despite its inanimate nature, we sure give the scale a lot of power to influence our lives.

Or perhaps you no longer have a scale, having abolished it from your life, convinced you don't need one. Consider this, however: not having a scale does not necessarily mean you've taken power back from the scale. If, when you go to the doctor's office, you insist that you "don't *do* scales," you may want to rethink how you think about the scale. The only way to know if a scale has no power over you is to step on it, read the data, and see what happens in your mind when you're up against the truth.

The thing is, we know damn well whether we're in a healthy weight range or an unhealthy weight range. In that sense, we don't *need* the scale to tell us anything. It's only there to give us factual feedback. It can't make us thinner or fatter. It merely tells us the truth about what we weigh. That is all. Why would we expect more from it?

When we approach the scale with trepidation, we have no business stepping on it because we aren't interested in the truth; we're actually hoping it will lie to us.

Which feels better? Unknowingly stepping on a broken scale that tells you that you weigh less than you really do, or stepping on a working scale that tells you that you actually (accurately) weigh a whole lot more?

Why?

Let's say you've been eating very poorly for the past few weeks or months. You know you've been overeating, and you know your food choices have been far from healthy. You decide to step on the scale, which indicates that you have indeed gained weight. You throw a fit. You decide it's going to be a bad day.

Why? What did the scale tell you that you didn't already know? What difference can fifteen seconds actually make (not counting what it can save you on car insurance)?

You see, when you focus on the scale and the *number*, you get to turn your back on your body and how you've been treating it. You can blame it all on the scale. Instead of using it as an informational tool, you use it as a way to not only continue to punish yourself, but also to distract you away from doing something

86

*for* your Self. The scale becomes just another way to abuse your body and not take responsibility for the abuse.

When the bathroom scale has the power to ruin your day, you'll have a hard time losing weight. You will be focusing on the wrong thing—the scale—and if it doesn't "make" you feel good, you will slip back into old habits of Self abuse.

## HUNGER IS YOUR BODY'S BUSINESS

Your body knows best. It tells you when to eat and when to stop eating. You don't get to *decide* to be physically hungry—that's your body's business. When it sends out a signal for food, no matter how hard your mind may try, it won't be able to change your body's "mind," because the human need for food is not optional. Attempts to ignore the body's natural hunger rhythms come with serious consequences, not the least of which is an overweight body.

Notwithstanding any medical conditions, when we eat according to our physical hunger cues, our bodies are able to maintain a "natural" healthy weight. It's what our bodies are designed to do. Eating what the body requires, instead of what the mind thinks it needs, can only have one outcome: the perfect weight for your body.

Have you lost touch with what physical hunger actually feels like in your body? Merely thinking you are hungry for food does not necessarily mean you are hungry *for food*, especially if you have trained your mind to override your body's hunger cues. You have taught your mind to confuse emotional hunger as a signal for food.

Physical hunger is a sensation that starts in your body and works its way up to your brain, which cues you that it's time to eat. If ignored for too long, the message becomes "DEFCON 1, code red, drop everything, and eat or things are going to get very ugly around here."

Emotional hunger, on the other hand, is a feeling that starts in your head and works its way down into your body. For example, you have the thought, "I don't want to be here," or "I'm all alone," which results in feelings of frustration or sadness. You can feel the sadness in your body as a result of the thought.

Generally speaking, if you feel your hunger below the neck, you are experiencing physical hunger. If you feel hunger above the neck, you are experiencing emotional hunger. Actual physical hunger starts in your stomach—it is a signal that your body needs food. Emotional hunger, on the other hand, starts in your mind, and no amount of food can feed it.

Another difference is that physical hunger comes on gradually, whereas emotional hunger comes on suddenly. Have you ever had a large meal, felt stuffed, and then took one look at the dessert being served and "felt" hungry again? That's emotional hunger, and it's often quickly followed up with a heaping helping of guilt.

If you look at the clock to determine whether it's time to eat, you are definitely not listening to your body's hunger cues; you're eating because "it's lunchtime" or because the food is there so you "may as well eat it."

But what if you were to wait for your body to tell you when it's time to eat? Asking your Self, "Why do I want to eat this right now?" is a crucial first step toward physical hunger awareness.

It's not uncommon for emotional eaters to lose touch with their bodies because they spend so much time "in their heads" creating thoughts that cause negative feelings, which are often confused with hunger, which leads to overeating. Getting reacquainted with her body requires that an emotional eater begin to listen for her body's *physical* hunger cues.

## BODY WHISPERING: LEARNING TO LISTEN SO YOUR BODY CAN TALK

If you want to attain and then maintain a healthy body weight, you're going to have to listen so your body can talk. In other words, you need to pay attention to your body's natural hunger signals instead of allowing your mind to override them.

Your body requires food for sustenance. Feed it what it *needs*, and it will return to its natural weight—not what's natural for someone else's body, but for *your* body.

What do you imagine it would be like if you only ate according to your body's needs? How much less do you think you would eat? Be prepared to be amazed.

Your body actually sends hunger signals to your brain when your stomach is empty. At first the signal is like a flutter in your belly, but make no mistake, it is a physical sensation and not an emotional vibration. Emotional eaters often confuse the two; that's why it's important to get back in touch with the language of your body.

At −2 there's no doubt about it; your body needs food. Your Dignity (if present) would not allow you to ignore your body, just as you would not allow someone you love to go hungry. Now is the time to eat the food you have prepared for your Self. If you don't eat now, you risk losing all control of your mind and are more likely to mistreat your body by eating whatever you can get your hands on and overfeeding it once you do start to eat.

At −3 your body's hunger signal becomes a roar, and your mind is no match for the increasingly intense physical sensation of hunger. It will take every ounce of willpower you have left (if any) in order to fight against your body. This isn't to say it can't be done; a well-trained mind can most certainly bring itself back from a short detour into the Land of WTF, but it's hard to stay rational when your body is threatening to mutiny.

Mutiny is almost certain at −4. By now your mind is lost in confusion, and all that matters is that you find something—anything— to eat. Whatever you may have promised your Self earlier (today I'm going to be "good") is long forgotten.

Your Dignity has left the building.

**◖◗**

Once again, to anyone who says that listening to her body is easier said than done, I would ask this: Do you think it is hard to have Dignity? Do you find it difficult to be in Integrity? If so, then you will think this work is easier said than done. But that's just a thought you've become accustomed to thinking. In truth, this is as easy as making a decision to take care of your Self, and then honoring that decision. Without resolve it will feel hard. Resolve makes *doing* this work easier. When we choose to think about how "hard" it is, we let ourselves off the hook, again and emotional (and gastrointestinal) mayhem is likely to ensue.

Look—I'm not saying this is easy peasy; I'm saying that with Dignity comes the willingness to do hard things when something important to you is at stake.

When you resolve to take back control of your mind you are in the Dignity Zone (i.e., in charge, in control, and at peace). You are putting your Self *first*.

If you are out of touch with your body's hunger signals, it may take a little practice to reconnect, but it won't be impossible. Sometimes we talk ourselves into thinking that things are much harder than they need to be. In part 2 of this book, there will be plenty of opportunities for practice.

Treating your body with Dignity means you don't make it wait to be fed; you eat when your "tank" feels empty but you still feel in control of your mind. Besides, why would you allow your body to be treated in any way other than dignified?

Fight for your body! It's worthy of all the love and care and attention in the world—especially from *you*. When you give it your attention, giving it the food (and exercise) it needs to perform at an optimal level, your body will respond; it knows what to do.

## READY TO MOVE ON TO STAGE 4?

Use the following checklist to determine whether you're ready for stage 4. Unless you can check them all, go back and review stage 3 before moving ahead.

☐ Fear and worry are beginning to loosen their grip on your mind.

☐ You believe in your own power and resilience.

☐ You're willing to start listening to your body's actual hunger signals.

☐ You accept responsibility for how much you weigh today.

☐ You trust that the Universe knows exactly what it's doing.

# STAGE 4

# Returning Home or "Look, Ma, My Ass is Shrinking!"

## INTEGRITY

Integrity brings you home to your Self. You have Integrity when you know what you stand for and then you stand up for it. If your actions tell a different story than the words coming out of your mouth, you are out of Integrity. Without Integrity, losing weight is a struggle, because for whatever reason, part of you is in resistance mode. You're in a fight against your Self. You're ignoring all signs and signals that you are mistreating your body and your Self.

When you're out of Integrity, something doesn't *feel* right.

Depending on which stage you're at in your weight loss journey, you will do one of the following four things.

1. Stay stuck in old and familiar (undignified) Think-Feel-Do patterns. This keeps you out of Integrity. One day you're on a diet, and the next day you're off, which only serves to perpetuate the cycle of Cry-Eat-Repeat. The call to adventure goes unheeded.

HONOR YOUR SELF

MOVE IT

TRUST YOUR BODY

DIET WITH LOVE

KNOW YOUR VALUES

KNOW THY SELF

You'll notice there are six layers to this cake. Don't think you can get away with just having the icing; you need all six layers.

**Layer 1:** Know (and trust) thy Self.

Your Self is not the part of you that thinks. Your Self is the part of you that *knows*. Your Self is deeply connected to your body and your soul, and she has only your best interests at heart. She's responsible, compassionate, and full of love for you; she's also extremely tolerant of your ego. Unlike your ego, however, she would never say mean things about you or to you. Your Self is the only one who can be trusted to tell you what to do but you have to be willing to create the space to listen. Slow down. Listening to your Self is also known as listening to your gut. Do more of that. Just listen. Ask, "What do I really want? What do I believe in? What do I value most? What feels like love in this moment?" And then wait for the answer. Create space for the answer to come to you.

**Layer 2:** Know what you stand for *and* stand up for it.

Like the thoughts in your head, talk is cheap—and potentially very fattening. Before you speak, listen to your Self in order to determine what's important to you—what you stand for—and then be prepared to stand up for it. Get very clear about your priorities. Know what you want, and if you don't know, find out. Go back to layer 1 and ask your Self. She knows. When you know what you really want, above all else, you won't be able to stop your Self from getting it.

**Layer 3:** Choose a diet that is approved by your Self.

As a card-carrying adult, you get to choose how to *think*, how to *feel*, and what to *do*. All. The. Time. That includes how you choose to Think-Feel-*Feed* your body. You can eat anything you want, as long as it feels like love. You can go on any diet you desire, even (especially!) if it includes cake. If your Self approves, you're good to go. Remember: whatever you choose to eat must feel good before, during, and after you eat it. It must be aligned with what you value most in life. If you feel guilt, you've skipped a layer of your Integrity Cake. You bypassed your Self.

**Layer 4:** Eat when you are hungry, and stop when you are full.

This layer requires that you respect your Self and trust your body by using the Dignity Hunger Scale. When you do this, you will know when it's "time" to eat. Then *eat*. Listen for your body to tell you when to stop. This takes practice, which you'll get a lot of in part 2 of this book.

**Layer 5:** Move your body—it's the dignified thing to do.

Your body needs to move. Not moving your body is unkind. Moving it in ways that don't feel good is undignified. So, if hopping on one foot while balancing an egg on your head feels good to you, then your Self approves. If hiking up and down hills doesn't feel good, don't do it. Your Self is the only one you have to answer to, so listen up when she tells you to haul ass. But do it in a way that feels like love.

**Layer 6:** *Above all else*, honor your Self and your body.

This is the thick layer of icing on top of your Integrity Cake. The reason people fall out of Integrity is because they don't put themselves first: they believe doing things for other people is "the nice (and proper) thing to do" even when it doesn't feel good to do it. Doing anything from a place other than love takes you out of Integrity. Being nice to others at the expense of your Self is not nice. If you want to be nice, then you must do so with Integrity, never with resentment. Here's an example:

Darcy's been invited to a party. She says she "doesn't know what to do," which is code for "I don't really want to go." Should she go or not go? Darcy thinks she only has two options when, actually, she has four:

1. Darcy could choose to not go to the party and be **out of Integrity**: In this scenario, Darcy feels very bad about her choice to not go. She thinks she's a "terrible friend." Her ego berates her. Darcy didn't even bother to listen to her Self; if she had, she would've chosen option 3.

2. Darcy could choose to go to the party and still be **out of Integrity** if she went unwillingly. In this scenario she tells herself that she "has to go" or else her friend will be upset. As a result, she goes but feels resentful. Darcy thinks it's the nice thing to do, but her Self doesn't buy it, hence, the resentment. Darcy is at war in her own head, and she's allowed her mind to trump her Self.

3. Darcy could choose to not go to the party and be **in Integrity**. If Darcy thought it truly would be best for her Self to not go to the party, even though it might upset her friend, she would be in Integrity because she would be honoring the needs of her Self. Darcy owns her choice to not go, even if her friend does get upset. Of course, she doesn't want to disappoint her friend, but she knows she can't control her friend's emotions.

4. Darcy could also choose to go to the party and be **in Integrity** even if she didn't really want to go. In this scenario, Darcy decides that it's worth going for the sake of her friend. She's willing to "suck it up" and go and her Self agrees. This means Darcy would feel good about her decision to go and there would be no resentment. This keeps her in Integrity.

As you can see, Darcy has two out of four opportunities to be in Integrity as she ponders whether to go to the party.

We always have choices. We just need to take the time to listen to our Self before we decide. In doing so we increase our chances of feeling good about our decisions.

And that is the crux of the Dignity Diet: making decisions that you can feel good about, even when it comes to food.

Let's change the scenario above and insert Twinkies for the party.

Darcy loves her Twinkies, but she knows they're hardly considered a nutritional powerhouse. Her best friend, who apparently thinks that Darcy "can't resist" Twinkies *and* who also knows how much Darcy struggles with her weight, often brings her a Twinkie as a "special treat." Darcy says she "doesn't know what to do"— should she eat the Twinkie so she doesn't hurt her friend's feelings or kick her friend in the shins? That's the burning question in her mind. Once again, Darcy thinks she only has two options—eat the damn Twinkie (and dishonor her Self) or don't eat it (and risk hurting her friend's feelings). In actuality, Darcy has four options:

1. Darcy could choose to not eat the Twinkie and be **out of Integrity**. In this scenario, Darcy feels tremendous angst about her choice to not eat the Twinkie. Not only does she think she's a "terrible friend," but her ego keeps taunting her to "just eat the stupid Twinkie and get it over with." Darcy's white knuckles are proof that she's using every ounce of willpower to fight the battle raging in her head. On top of that, she's wilting under the glare of her "offended" friend. No one wins—not even the Twinkie.

2. Darcy could choose to eat the Twinkie and still be **out of Integrity**. Here, Darcy "feels bad" for her friend, who "went to all that trouble to buy the damn Twinkie." She would tell herself that she "has to eat it" in order to keep her friend from feeling hurt. As a result, Darcy eats it but feels resentful. Darcy's mind tells her, "It's the nice thing to do." Mayday! Darcy is at war in her own head, and she's allowed her mind to trump her Self who's been trying to tell her that, in this instance, not eating the Twinkie is the loving thing to do. Damn those Twinkies!

3. Darcy could choose to not eat the Twinkie and be **in Integrity**. If Darcy listened to her higher Self and chose not to eat the Twinkie, even though it might upset her friend, she would be in Integrity because she would be honoring her Self and her body first. Besides, it's her friend's business if she chooses to be upset—it's not Darcy's job to control how her friend chooses to react. Darcy feels good about her choice to not eat the Twinkie, even if her friend chooses to get all tied up in a knot of thought-induced hurt.

4. Darcy could choose to eat the Twinkie and still be **in Integrity**. In order to be in Integrity Darcy would have to want to eat the Twinkie and then eat the Twinkie without a chaser of guilt. That last part is where it gets tricky: Integrity and guilt don't mix. Unlike her Child Mind, which doesn't concern itself with Integrity—it wants what it wants, and it wants it *pronto*—Darcy could ask her Self if eating the Twinkie would feel like a loving thing to do. If the answer is yes, Darcy could decide that on *this* occasion she will eat the Twinkie, with glee. This keeps her in Integrity.

As long as Darcy remains unaware of options three and four, the ones that would keep her in Integrity, she will find herself locked in a double bind in her own mind, which is bound to keep her stuck in Stage 1.

# TESTING YOUR INTEGRITY

As you now know, Integrity is about knowing what you stand for *and* being willing to stand up for it. Notice, that's a two-part test. In other words, just saying you really want to lose weight or that being healthy is important to you doesn't mean squat unless you take action that is consistent with what you say. Just saying you really want to lose weight without taking action means you are out of Integrity. Don't get me wrong: you can choose to not take action and still be in Integrity—that's similar to option 3 above. In other words, modify your "want" so that you are in Integrity. It feels better. The truth always feels better.

Saying, "I want to lose weight, but I'm not willing to take action right now," is a much more honest and truthful statement than saying the first part and ignoring the action part.

Here are your four TFD options when it comes to losing weight:

1.  Think: "I *have to* go on a diet."

    Feel: Resistance

    Do: Maintain status quo (continue to mindlessly overeat)

    **= No Integrity**

2.  Think: "My body is disgusting."

    Feel: Guilt, Shame

    Do: Use willpower to restrict food intake

    **= No Integrity**

3.  Think: "I'm learning a new way to think about my body,
    food, and weight."

    Feel: Acceptance

    Do: Make reclaiming your Dignity and reconnecting
    with your Self a priority.

    **= Integrity**

4.  Think: "I'm ready to lose weight."

    Feel: Inspired

    Do: Follow a dignified diet that feels like love

    **= Integrity**

Throughout this book I've been encouraging you to move from options one and two, which are indicative of stage 1 "stuckness," to options three and four, because Integrity feels good.

When what you think feels good, that's an indication that you are aligned with your Self. What you choose to *do* is entirely up to you, and it's no one else's business what you ultimately decide.

Aligning your Think-Feel-Do with what you say is important to you is like having your Integrity Cake and eating it too.

# WHAT'S YOUR (SOB) STORY?

The mind loves a good story. And by "good" I mean lousy, stinkin', *rotten*. The mind likes to keep itself very busy by telling the same damn story over and over and *over* again. Child Mind in particular is an expert sob story teller. But before you try to do a rewrite, it's a good idea to take a careful read of your story: it has a lot to tell you about who you think you are.

Think of your story as the software that's been downloaded (by your parents, teachers, siblings, *Alvin and the Chipmunks*) into your operating system, also known as your Belief System (such an appropriate acronym). Here's the thing: when you tell yourself a lousy BS story, it's bound to have a lousy ending.

## HOW KAT GOT HER STORY BACK

Telling your story to your Self can be a fascinating, eye-opening process.

I always have my coaching clients tell me their stories because it is so revealing—*to them* as well as to me. I cannot tell you how often I am told, "I had no idea I had all that going on in my head."

Let me tell you about Kat, who hired me to coach her "to lose weight so she could be happy and attract a man and get married." It went like this:

> My parents were very strict when I was growing up, and when I was in fifth grade my dad said I was getting a little chubby so my mom took me to Weight Watchers. Can you imagine: What kind of mother takes her kid to Weight Watchers? It was awful and I was hungry and unhappy all the time, except when I would go to my friend's house, and her mom would give us cookies and potato chips whenever we wanted. Needless to say, I pretty much stayed chubby, which really pissed off my dad because he would say stuff to me like, "Why can't you be like a normal kid?" It made me feel like such a loser. My mother was always walking on eggshells when it came to my dad, so she would never defend me or anything. When I went to college, I gained the freshmen fifteen and the sophomore seventeen, then the junior gigantonormous. By the time I was in my senior year, I was so afraid of gaining any more weight (my dad said he would no longer pay my tuition if I dared gain one more pound), I decided to eat and purge. I also took up running. Run. Eat. Purge. Run. Eat. Purge. It worked, and I lost thirty-six pounds in about five months. The look on my dad's face when he saw me "shrinking down" made me feel like I had finally done something "right." Bulimia saved me from the wrath of my father. Of course, I eventually got sick. Short story: I went into therapy, stopped purging, and now I'm up thirty pounds. My dad says I'll never get a man looking like this, and I guess he's right. I've had a couple of boyfriends, but the relationships never last. I can't say I blame them. Who'd want a fat girl like me, right? So, it's time to lose this weight once and

for all, so I can make everybody happy, including myself, if that's even possible. Besides, I really would like to get married someday, if anyone will have me.

What do you imagine Kat "feels" like on a day-to-day basis? Do you assume she's unhappy?

When I asked her, she said she was "pretty happy" *except* for the fact that she was overweight, didn't have a boyfriend, and was always fighting with her father. Other than that, life was great.

*Veddy inteddesting,* don't you think?

When I asked Kat why she thought she was overweight, she looked at me as if I had two heads.

"Because I want to protect myself from getting hurt," she said.

"So, nothing ever hurts you now?" I asked.

She thought about that for a minute or two and then said, "Well, yes, things still hurt me. People can be so hurtful. They say mean things. Maybe I'm just sensitive."

I pressed a little. "So, then the extra weight does or does not protect you?"

"I guess not," she said, sounding rather defeated, as if I'd just cut her parachute rip cord.

"OK then, why are you overweight?"

"Um, I think it's because it pisses off my dad."

"Really!"

Long pause. Very long pause.

I pressed on. "Really? Is that why you're overweight—so you can piss off your dad?"

"Is this a trick question?" she demanded.

"Nope."

"I have no idea why I'm overweight," she finally said, exasperated.

By this point I think Kat would've strangled *me* with a rip cord if she'd had one handy. I wasn't buying into her story, and she was perplexed because people usually love hearing her story. They would always nod in agreement and help Kat coddle her story. Her story was like an adorable little puppy: everyone wanted to pet it.

Except me.

And I was starting to get the impression that she wanted a different reaction from me.

"I think it's important to understand why you're overweight, don't you?" I asked.

"Well, you seem to have all the answers, so why don't you just tell me?"

It was time to pull out my velvet gloves—the ones with the invisible brass knuckles.

"Kat, I think you're overweight because you overeat."

"Well, duh-uh, of course I overeat! I didn't need to hire you to tell me that!"

"Then why did you tell me you're overweight because it protected you from being hurt? And because you wanted to piss off your dad?"

"And your point is?" she asked, her fists starting to clench.

"My point is, I'm confused, and I suspect you are too. Which is it? Protection? Your dad? Overeating?"

"Overeating. There. Satisfied? I'm such a loser."

Ah yes: the Hail Mary comment. She threw it out there, praying I would finally buy into her sad loser story.

She picked the wrong coach for that.

"Kat, you are overweight because you overeat. That's the good news. Fantastic news, actually. It's not because of something that is out of your control. Or because of what someone did to you. Or because there's something wrong with you. Which isn't to say bad things didn't happen to you in the past. But when we tell ourselves a story about why we are overweight *today*, and we say it's because of what happened in the past, we give up all our power to attain the body we say we want. Every time you eat when you are not hungry, it's because you make the decision to overeat. No one makes you overeat. Can you own that?"

"Um, I guess so. I'm confused."

I proceeded to explain to Kat that the reason she was overweight was the same reason she overate: the story she tells herself today about what happened in the past. It's a lousy story, and it makes her want to cry, and then eat, then repeat. Kat's story made her feel all kinds of emotions: sadness, anger (toward her dad), resentment (toward her mother), and loneliness (whenever she "gets dumped" by a boyfriend). But rather than deal with the painful emotions she creates in her mind, Kat chose to avoid them by stuffing them down with food. Then she felt guilty and ashamed for having done so. In effect, she traded one set of painful emotions for another.

It was a vicious cycle, to say the least.

Kat's overeating was driven by the negative emotions caused by the negative story that ran through her mind, even when she thought she wasn't thinking about it. That's the problem with these stories, they never change, and they never end.

Our emotions are driven by a set of belief constructs that were established a long time ago by our primary programmers and influencers—the people in our lives who had power to shape the way we think: parents, teachers, friends, and the stuff we watched on TV. As children we believed what we were told, and we also made up a lot of nonsense because our minds weren't capable of making sense of some of the things that happened around us. Those beliefs formed the basis of our stories. Our stories, which roam freely in our minds *all the time*, are often tied up in negative emotion. That's why our stories often *suck*.

I asked Kat how old she felt that day when she told her story, and she was quick to answer—eight. She said she often felt like an eight-year-old girl trapped in the body of a thirty-two-year-old woman. As we worked together, Kat could see how she had abdicated all responsibility for how she fed her body currently. While overeating may have been a logical coping skill for an eight-year-old, as an adult, Kat had always had the power to make different choices.

In order to rewrite her story, Kat first had to understand that it was her story to write and that she could write it any way she damn well pleased. While the facts and circumstances of her life might not have been in her control when she was a child, the thoughts and beliefs (and occasional hyperbole) she clung to as an adult did not serve her.

Let's take a look at Kat's story again, but this time, let's strike out anything that isn't factual. We want just the facts, ma'am, just the facts.

My parents ~~were very strict when I was growing up, and~~ when I was in fifth grade my dad said I was getting a little chubby so my mom took me to Weight Watchers. ~~Can you imagine: What kind of mother takes her kid to Weight Watchers? It was awful and I was hungry and unhappy all the time, except when~~ I would go to my friend's house and her mom would give us cookies and potato chips ~~whenever we wanted. Needless to say, I pretty much~~ stayed chubby, ~~which really pissed off my dad because~~ he would say stuff to me like, "Why can't you be like a normal kid?" ~~It made me feel like such a loser. My mother was always walking on eggshells when it came to my dad so she would never defend me or anything.~~ When I went to college I gained the freshmen fifteen, and the sophomore seventeen, then the junior ~~gigantonormous~~ (twenty-two). ~~By the time~~ I was in my senior year ~~I was so afraid of gaining any more weight~~ (my dad said he would no longer pay my tuition if I dared gain one more pound) so I decided to eat and purge. I also took up running. ~~Run. Eat. Purge. Run. Eat. Purge. It worked, and~~ I lost thirty-six pounds in about five months. ~~The look on my dad's face when he saw me "shrinking down" made me feel like I had finally~~

done something "right." Bulimia saved me from the wrath of my father. Of course, I eventually got sick. Short story: I went into therapy, stopped purging, and now I'm up thirty pounds. My dad says I'll never get a man looking like this, and I guess he's right. I've had a couple of boyfriends, but the relationships never last. I can't say I blame them. Who'd want a fat girl like me, right? So, it's time to lose this weight, once and for all, so I can make everybody happy, including myself, if that's even possible. Besides, I really would like to get married someday, if anyone will have me.

Kat didn't really like what I did to her (sob) story. She argued and fought to put just about everything back in. She said it was all fact, as sure as the world is flat.

The reason we fight to keep our stories is because we don't know who we are without them. Whenever our belief systems get rattled, we run. Why? Because we've spent our whole lives believing what we were programmed to believe: "My mother shouldn't have taken me to Weight Watchers," "My dad was too strict and mean," and "I can't get a man because I'm fat." Without a belief system to fall back on, no matter how warped and twisted, we feel lost. We don't know who we are. We don't know what to *do*. The default belief is "this is just the way it is; this is who I am."

But what if Kat's programming had mostly been wrong? What if Kat's primary influencers did what they did because their own operating systems were corrupted? And what if Kat's Child Mind misinterpreted the reasons behind her parents' and other people's behavior?

What if...

- Kat's father had no idea how to connect to a child, even his own daughter? (Kat said he had never had a loving connection with his own parents.)
- Kat's mother took her to Weight Watchers because she loved her daughter and was worried about her health, and she wanted to do *something*, and that's the only thing she could think of?
- Kat's relationships with men ended because they had to? After all, they were unhealthy and she didn't yet know how to attract someone with whom she could be in a healthy relationship.

Is the following story not as plausible as Kat's original sob-fortified version?

> My parents had no clue how to be parents, and I don't want to blame them for that—blaming is too easy. I know they loved me. My mom took me to Weight Watchers because she and my dad were worried about my weight—for whatever reason, But when I see myself in pictures I don't think I was overweight back then. I wasn't rail thin, but I wasn't "abnormal." I am overweight now because I continue to overeat for emotional reasons, but I am learning how to be kind to myself, and that includes not feeding my body when it isn't hungry. I have no idea how to be in a relationship with a man, and that's OK; I'm learning about that too. My story doesn't end here. It's just beginning.

When I offered Kat this version of her story, her demeanor changed instantly. She leaned forward. She actually seemed to like this story—and, suddenly, *me*.

Kat quickly realized that this new and improved story could be *as true or truer* than her old one. And she admitted that it certainly felt better, emotionally speaking. In fact, Kat said it felt more "peaceful." It actually felt more like the truth than her old story.

Kat also realized something big: she'd been playing the role of a helpless victim. Since the V word didn't taste very good in her mouth, Kat spit it out once and for all. And then she said:

> "I think I was always hoping that food
> would make the taste of 'victim' go away."

SHAZZAM, Batman! I had to write that one down. It was clear that Kat was well on her way to getting her Dignity back. The rewrite we did of her story reflected her willingness to take responsibility (the bottom layer of the Dignity Sandwich) for where she was today and how she got here. She could own the facts of her life without adding drama and meaning that didn't belong and served no purpose. She could take responsibility for her body, her relationships, and her job. She did *not* have to take responsibility for her parents' (un)happiness, or anyone else's for that matter, by doing what they expected of her. She began to see how her new and responsible choices might actually piss her parents off.

And that would be OK. That would be *their* choice.

This is how Kat eventually rewrote her story:

> My name is Kat and I am thirty-two years old. I am an adult woman. I am no longer an eight-year-old in my mind. I am 5'4" and I weigh 168 pounds. I am an accountant. I love to read, garden and play board games. As an adult I make my own decisions and take responsibility for the outcome of those decisions. I have parents, and I'm working on

redefining my relationship with them. I love them, and I am learning to establish boundaries in order to honor my Self when it comes to interacting with them and anyone else who thinks they know what's best for me. I realize I am the one who gets to decide who I want to be in my life. I am currently dating a kindhearted man. I don't know where this relationship will lead, and I'm 100 percent OK with not knowing. I have learned to trust my Self above all else. I am following a diet I love, and I'm also moving my ass around the block five days a week. So, this is what it feels like to be a grown-up!

Now there's a story that will *serve* Kat. It has Dignity and Integrity. And best of all, it *feels* good to Kat when she tells it to her Self, over and over and *over* again.

## HOW TO TELL A BETTER STORY

When someone says to you, "Tell me about yourself," what do you say? What's the first thing you think of?

Do you say, "I am a creature of incredible awesomeness"?

Who do you think you are?

Whatever it is you may think about you, you can be sure it's tied to the story you tell yourself (in your head) all day long.

Is your story like Kat's original sob fest, full of false assumptions and hurtful conclusions? Who or what have you been blaming for what's "wrong" with you and your life? What old thoughts and beliefs do you still carry with you that shape the way you present your Self to the world?

Take a moment now to tell your story without censoring: write it all down, the good, the bad, and the sob. Don't worry—no one has to read it but you, but it's important that you actually write it down in "thought dump" fashion. Now is not the time to start the rewrite.

Here are some questions to help you get started:

- Who do you think you are? Describe you in detail.
- What were you like as a child? Why?
- What is the same or different about you as a child and you as an adult?
- Describe your relationship with your mother. What things stick out most in your mind about her? What things stick out most in your mind about the way she treated you?
- Describe your relationship with your father. What things stick out most in your mind about him? What things stick out most in your mind about the way he treated you?
- If you had a close and healthy relationship with your parents, describe a difficult relationship you had in the past. Why was this relationship difficult for you? What did you Think-Feel-Do back then when you were around this person? Why?
- What impressions do you have of yourself today? Where did you learn to think about you this way?

## MY STORY: JUST THE FACTS

Now, go back and read your story and cross out anything that is not based in *fact*. If it helps, take a look at all the things we crossed out of Kat's story as an example: if it's not *provable in court* then it's got to go. Write down what's left below. Be sure to add any missing facts, such as "I am a _____-year-old woman. I weigh _____ pounds."

Notice if it was difficult for you to deal with the facts and nothing but the facts. Stay curious. You'll have another chance to rewrite your amazing story in part 2 of this book.

## SELF CARE DEFINED

Self care is quite possibly *the one thing* that we don't get right on a day-to-day basis. I think it's because we confuse Self care with *action*—doing things to take care of ourselves. On the contrary, Self care happens in the mind: it's your ability to remain conscious and aware of your thoughts and emotions, no matter what is happening in the world around you. Self care protects your Dignity and keeps you in Integrity.

Self care, therefore, is *not* about going for a massage or a mani-pedi or indulging in your favorite foods; those are *things you do*. True Self care puts an emphasis on feeling better first and *then* treating yourself to whatever your heart desires. Dignity and Integrity are always your top priorities. A mani-pedi ought to be the extra cheese in your Dignity Sandwich or the icing on your Integrity Cake.

Whenever you choose to "treat" yourself to make up for feeling badly about something that's happening in your life, you put your Integrity on hold. For example, let's say you have decided that your physical health is a top priority. In order to have Integrity, you would have to follow up with the actions that support this priority. If, however, you have a "hard day at the office" and choose to eat in a way that is inconsistent with the priority of improving your health, then your Integrity is—how shall we say this—*kaput*.

Self care is Integrity's chief operating officer. It requires that you stand up for all the things you say are important to you, including your deepest desires, your unique little quirks, your utterly adorable expressions, your irrepressible creativity, and your fundamental goodness.

When we don't take care of our Self, we shortchange the world. Instead, we ought to fill ourselves up to the point of overflowing because it's the overflow that we give to others that is far more valuable than anything we give when we're feeling exhausted, resentful, or just plain unhappy.

Think about it: If I show up tired and frazzled to be with you (because I'm trying to be nice), is that actually fair to you? Is it not undignified of me to show up as a fragment of the person I am capable of being (not to mention how *not fun* it would be for you)? When I fail to take good care of my Self, I cannot be the best mother I can be, I cannot be the best wife I can be, and I cannot be the best friend I can possibly be. Everyone loses out.

## METACOGNITION: THE KEY TO SELF CARE

Metacognition is the key to getting your bigger-than-you-want-it-to-be ass to happy, *now*. As a human being you are capable of watching your mind think—no other creature on the planet can do that. Here's why this is important: when you step back and observe your mind, you are able to connect with your true Self—that part of you that is so damn devoted to You that it makes me want to cry. (Don't worry; I'll get over it.)

Metacognition takes you beyond mere thought level (where your mind is often in control of you) to a connection with your Self. When you detach from your thoughts, your mind is cleared of clutter, giving your Self an opportunity to decide what's best for You.

# ASS-SHRINKING TOOL #2: THE INTEGRITY SCALE

Along with a fuel gauge, your car has a tachometer, which measures how fast the engine is revving at any given speed. Similarly, the Integrity Scale[2] measures the speed at which your body is "revving" in order to determine how conscious and aware you are at any given moment in time. This draws on your uniquely human ability to think about what you're thinking about. Our thoughts and emotions emit vibrations that are either positive or negative. The Integrity Scale may very well be the greatest ass-shrinking tool ever invented (hyperbole duly noted) because it forces you to *woman up* and take responsibility for the thoughts you choose to think, the feelings those thoughts create, and the actions you take as a result. When your actions match your priorities, you are in Integrity.

**The Integrity Scale: Measuring Conscious Awareness**

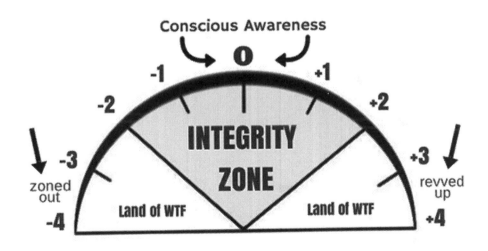

---

[2] If you'd like to download and print out a copy of the Integrity Scale, visit www.LinEleoff.com

The Integrity Scale measures your level of conscious awareness from −4 (zoned out) at one end to **+4** (revved up) on the other. Either extreme takes you into the Land of WTF and out of conscious awareness.

On the negative end of the scale, between −2 and −4, the unpracticed mind shuts itself down as a means of Self protection. When this happens we become emotionally "unavailable." It's a childlike way of coping with emotions we don't want to feel. By shutting off the mind and its thoughts, the intensity of the emotion is reduced. We may describe it as "zoning out" or "checking out." Welcome to the Land of WTF. Zombies love it here.

On the plus side of the scale (between +2 and +4), the mind is revving itself up—our thoughts seem to have hitched onto a runaway train, and that means the emotion being experienced is also getting revved up. We may describe this as feeling out of control or becoming "extremely emotional," whether we're experiencing happiness or sadness. Remember, this is about being conscious of what's happening in the mind; it's not about the emotion itself.

Cognitive awareness diminishes whether you experience a positive or negative emotion. The more heightened the emotion, the less "conscious" you become.

Ideally, we want to stay conscious more often than not in order to maintain control of our mind (and its thoughts). Dignity—the belief that we are a fundamental force in the Universe—is the impetus behind our Integrity. Our Dignity inspires awareness, which keeps us in Integrity. Between −2 and +2 we are in the Integrity Zone; even at −2, when we're starting to feel as though we just want to turn it all off, or at +2 when we can feel that we're getting revved up, we still have the presence of mind to stand up for what we believe to be right and good according to our Self.

Don't get me wrong: this doesn't mean we're in the Land of La-Dee-Da, but rather that we are consciously creating a mind state that is useful. Whether it's anger or sadness, peace or joy, we are present in the moment; we are dealing with and in control of our (very human) emotions. That's the Integrity Zone.

It is where we *deal*.

It's really important to understand that this is not an emotional scale, but rather a *consciousness* scale—the more conscious and aware we are, the more we can stay in control of everything we think, feel, and do. For example, if we allow our anger to go beyond +2, then we are more likely to step out of Integrity with our actions—we're too revved up to think clearly. The same goes for excitement: if you were to find out you'd just won the lottery, you'd likely push the Integrity meter to +4; there's no hope in hell you'd be able to figure out what you're going to do with that money until you calm your mind.

If what we value is a calm and rational means of resolving life's problems, then we should aim to hold ourselves in the Integrity Zone most of the time. It's not that we shouldn't feel anger, but rather that we are conscious enough to be able to "listen" to what our anger is trying to teach us. This takes mental and emotional fortitude, and the closer we can keep to 0, where the mind is idling smoothly, the more rational and thoughtful we will be no matter what emotion we're experiencing.

## HOW TO USE THE INTEGRITY SCALE WHEN YOU'RE ON THE DIGNITY DIET

Remember, the Dignity Diet starts with losing the fat in your head and ends with losing the fat on your ass.

First, get clear about what is *most important* to you when it comes to your body, your health, and your overall fitness level. Once you're clear on your priorities, write down what you would have to *think*, how you would have to *feel*, and what you would have to *do* to honor your priorities and stay in the Integrity Zone.

For example…

Priority #1: Reclaim my Dignity while honoring my Self and my body.

In order to honor this priority I would have to…

> Think: "I am worth taking care of, and my body deserves my attention more than it deserves a donut."
>
> Feel: Resolve. Motivation.
>
> Do: Choose foods wisely and responsibly; exercise/move my body at least five days a week for thirty minutes.
>
> Outcome: Integrity.

Priority # 2: Lose ten pounds.

In order to honor this priority I would have to…

> Think: "I am willing to do whatever it takes to lose the weight in my head by dieting with Dignity and honoring my Self."
>
> Feel: Empowered. In control. At peace.
>
> Do: Pay attention to the thoughts in my head; separate the truth (facts) from the fiction that is my sob story.

I make choices that are aligned with my priority to lose weight.

Outcome: Integrity.

Do this exercise for *no more than two priorities* at a time. Use the Integrity Scale to make sure you're consciously aware of the thoughts running through your mind at any given moment. Be careful not to let your mind catch a runaway train in either direction, positive or negative, or you'll lose control of your thoughts, and, with them, your emotions. And we all know that wherever your emotions go, your actions are quick to follow.

## FAT-FREE FEELINGS

Fat-free feelings are a staple of the Dignity Diet. You cannot have too many of them. Some fat-free feelings can also be very "nutrient-dense" because they create a sort of snowball effect—the more you feel them, the better you feel. Oddly enough, they tend to be excellent calorie burners. Fat-free feelings are also a sign that you are in the Integrity Zone. Put these feelings on your "all-you-can-*feel*" list.

Although nothing is ever "forbidden" on the Dignity Diet, there are some feelings that are so full of fat they take you beyond the Integrity Zone and will require your extra-special attention in order for you to make room for fat-free-feeling alternatives.

The following "Feel This" column of feelings can be experienced with Integrity. The "Not This" feelings definitely take you out of the Integrity Zone.

| Feel This (Fat-Free Emotions) | Not This (Full Fat) |
|---|---|
| Loving | Hateful |
| Peaceful | Resentful |
| Happy | Miserable |
| Joyful | Despairing |
| Accepting | Resisting |
| Motivated | Helpless |
| Inspired | Empty |
| Grateful | Entitled |
| Kindhearted | Meanspirited |
| Optimistic | Disillusioned |
| Hopeful | Hopeless |
| Worthy | Worthless |
| Compassionate | Apathetic |
| Confident | Inferior |
| Admiring | Jealous |
| Willing | Unwilling |

When you're feeling a negative emotion that you can't get your-self out of, curiosity will almost always get you back into the Integrity Zone. Simply ask, "What other way can I think about this that feels a little better?" This takes back control over your mind.

## FEELING WITH INTEGRITY

There are going to be emotions that don't feel good but are nev-ertheless necessary to your personal growth and healing. These emotions are triggered by AFGOs—life events that have the potential to send us reeling in pain. However, while the pain of loss is natural, it's important to allow your Self to feel your emo-tions with Integrity; in other words, if you are grieving the loss of a loved one, your mind may also be tempted to ramp up those emotions by thinking thoughts that are not helpful. "It shouldn't have happened" is a very common and painful thought that does not lead to healing.

Feelings such as anger, sadness, fear, loss, and even anxiety can actually serve you, but only when allowed to flow *through* you with Integrity—this means they are accompanied by *acceptance* with the way things are in your life right now, by a *willingness* to work through the feelings, and with *awareness* rather than just slapping the "hunger" feeling label on them and then stuffing them down with food. The Integrity Scale will be an important tool as you embark on the Dignity Diet, and the more you are able to hang out in the Integrity Zone, the less likely you are to mistake your emotions for hunger. That's because, well, quite simply, you've got better things to do, and you'll feel like doing them.

## READY TO MOVE ON TO PART 2?

Use the following checklist to determine whether you're ready for "Part 2: The Dignity Diet." Unless you can check them all, go back and review stages 1 through 4 before moving ahead.

- ☐ You are ready to step into the Integrity Zone.

- ☐ You have a feeling that your sob story is very fattening.

- ☐ You no longer want to blame your parents for your current reality.

- ☐ You've become an expert at making the Dignity Sandwich.

- ☐ You're ready to make room for your Adult Mind to take charge.

# PART 2

# The Dignity Diet in Action—Here We Go!

*You are worthy, you are enough, you matter.*
*Believe this with your whole heart and soul*
*and you will have reclaimed your Dignity.*

Get ready to start taking action, because merely reading about the Dignity Diet won't get you very far.

This is your opportunity to implement what you learned in part 1. This is where I walk you through each of the four stages on your weight loss journey. I'm never going to tell you that it's easy, but if you've got even an ounce of curiosity on your plate, you've got everything you need. Wait. You need a spiral notebook—nothing fancy schmancy is required (although fancy schmancy is welcome, too, if that's how you want to rock and roll for the next six weeks).

Bring your AFGO Notebook with you everywhere. Think of it as an extension of your Self rather than a loathsome journal you "have to" fill out every day. C'mon, put your big girl shoes on,

Mama. 'Cause you want this, right? This is not going to be some effortless walk in the park: we're on a mission to get your Dignity back so that you can get your Integrity back so that you can get your *body* back, all in that order. It's important that you put your whole Self in, "hokey-pokey" style, 'cause that's what it's all about, dammit.

But hey—you absolutely can turn back, and if you're not ready, I strongly encourage you to go back to the stage in the book where you think you got stuck. I'll walk you through it again. But you should know this: the Dignity Diet *starts where you are* and takes you where you are *ready* to go.

The Dignity Diet is a six-week/forty-two-day action plan designed to get your mind clean and lean and your ass slim and trim. But who says you "have to" do it in six weeks? Maybe you need twelve weeks—or maybe you'll want to start over after week three. If you're doing the Dignity Diet the way you're supposed to, then you'll embrace the notion that there's no such thing as "supposed to."

Just be sure to do this one thing—get a spiral notebook or bunch of paper held together in any manner you choose, call it your AFGO Notebook, and record your journey. You'll thank me later because your notes will become the greatest gift from your Self to your Self, especially on those days where you just want to say "#$%& it."

Each day you are encouraged to do the "AFGO HOMEWORK" for that day. You'll be asked a lot of questions—please keep an open mind and resist the temptation to skip over the ones you find uncomfortable; those are the ones you need to answer *the most*.

Your job is to:

1. Fill in the blanks and/or answer the questions presented.

2. Add your own comments and observations.

3. Know exactly *why* you may choose to *not* do any or all of the above.

Are you ready to take back control of your mind?

Are you prepared to take care of your body?

Are you willing to reconnect with your Self?

If so, then *here we go...*

# WEEK 1

# YOU ARE *WORTHY,* YOU ARE *ENOUGH,* YOU *MATTER*

The Dignity Diet is really about feeding your Self what you've really been craving your whole life: Validation. Love. Attention. A sense of Self worth. You can't get those feelings from food.

Not even the most deliciously decadent chocolate chip cookie can ever validate your existence.

The world's best pizza is simply not able to love you back.

That half-caff-laff-naff pumpkin-spice turbo-charged latté is never going to "make it all go away."

That's *your* job, my new best friend, and hopefully you realize it's time for you to at least start to entertain the notion that you're worth it. You are worth fighting for. Your body is worth your attention.

This first week of the Dignity Diet is about getting to really *know* your Self. You have been fighting a war in your head for a very long time. It's time to surrender. Besides, I have a feeling your Self is more than you ever imagined.

# DAY 1: GETTING MOTIVATED

Motivation comes from a decision you make *in your mind* to do something you believe will be good for your Self. It may require some (gentle) pushing and prodding on your part. Getting motivated often requires some willpower as a kick-start to taking action when we truly believe that the action is in our best interests (But we say we "can't be bothered"). Motivation will only get us so far, however, because, as we already know, willpower is a limited resource—we cannot sustain it forever. However, it can absolutely be used to our advantage.

Inspiration, on the other hand, comes from willingness power—an unlimited resource—and it picks up where motivation leaves off. I guess you could say motivation inspires inspiration, but that sounds weird. Inspiration comes *from the heart,* and it's available on an all-you-can-use basis. You'll know when you've shifted from motivation to inspiration because you'll feel your creative energy start to flow through you: weight loss will be just the beginning of the many natural consequences that come with honoring your Self.

Don't worry if you're not yet feeling inspired to take action; that's OK. All you really need at this point is to feel motivated, even just a little, to start taking action. Soon, your motivation will morph into inspiration, and you'll feel like a bird that has been set free from her cage.

Keep in mind that the foundation of the Dignity Diet is to respect your Self and trust your body. Remember, putting your Self first is the most Self*less* thing you can do because, as you step into your authenticity, you have so much more to give to the ones you love and the world at large. This isn't about relegating everyone else to the back of the bus; this is about *driving* the bus so that you can take the ones you love on the ride of a lifetime.

There is nothing you deserve more than your own Self care. There is nothing the world needs more than your authentically dignified (and soon-to-be-shrinking) ass.

AFGO HOMEWORK:

1. List all the reasons why you say you *want* to go on the Dignity Diet.

2. Beside each reason, which is a thought, name the exact feeling you feel when you think this thought.

3. List all the reasons why you haven't lost weight and kept it off in the past.

4. Beside each of those reasons, name the exact feeling you feel when you tell your Self this.

5. List all the thoughts that motivate you to get started. (Use whatever thoughts you can muster to get going.)

# DAY 2: CREATING A JUDGMENT-FREE ZONE, PART 1

You're probably becoming aware of the manner in which you've been talking to your Self on a regular basis. Too often we aren't even aware of the subversive, abusive thoughts that linger just below the surface of our conscious mind.

Our judgments, not only of our Self but also of others, are fattening. Judgmental is one of those feelings that serve no purpose when the judgments are unkind.

Today you are invited to eavesdrop on your mind. Pay particular attention to the judgments you make and what purpose they serve. When you judge your Self, how does that make you feel?

Allow your Self to show you where you hurt.

AFGO HOMEWORK:

1. List all the unkind judgments you pass on your Self from the moment you wake up today until you go to bed tonight.

2. Beside each judgment, which is a thought, *not a fact,* explain why you think this way. How long have you felt this way about your Self?

3. Who else do you judge and why? List all the unkind judgments you pass on others.

4. Beside each judgment, which is a thought, *not a fact,* explain why you think this way about each person.

What else did you notice today?

# DAY 3: CREATING A JUDGMENT-FREE ZONE, PART 2

Today, make a promise that you will never again say an unkind word about *you* to your Self. No more Self flagellation. Think about it: How likely are you to do something well for someone who berates you, talks behind your back (Oh yes you do!), and completely ignores you when you need her most? The only way to get your Self on board the Dignity Diet is with kindness.

Today, write an apology letter to your Self. Tell her all the things you're sorry for and why.

Explain to your Self why you thought it would be OK to say these things to her. Where did you learn to think this way about You?

Here's how to apologize:

Step 1. A heartfelt apology begins with taking responsibility for the hurtful things you've said. This is a crucial first step toward forgiveness.

Step 2. Next, show that you understand what the repercussions have been; explain that you understand the results of your Self judgment.

Step 3. Ask your Self for forgiveness, and as much as you can, tell your Self exactly what you are willing to do to remedy the situation.

AFGO HOMEWORK:

*Dear Self,*

I am truly sorry for:

The reasons, as I understand them, are because:

I learned to think of my Self this way when:

I wholeheartedly take responsibility for:

I understand that the repercussions are:

I ask for your forgiveness because:

And I am willing to:

So that I can make things right between us.

# DAY 4: OBSERVING YOUR SELF WHEN YOU EAT

Today, pay special attention to the *way* you eat. This means being aware of everything you think, feel, and do, before, during, and after you eat.

**Before you put any food in your mouth**, notice your thoughts. Be very specific. How did you decide it was time to eat? How did you decide what you would eat? What are your thoughts about the food? What are your thoughts about your Self? What are you feeling?

What position is your body in? Standing? Sitting? Where?

Once you begin to eat, notice your thoughts as you chew the food. What does it really taste like—better or worse than you expected? Be very specific. What are your thoughts about your Self? What are you *feeling* as you're eating?

How did you know when to stop eating?

Do this every time you eat something today, no matter how big or small. Do not censor your eating habits. The goal is awareness, *not change.*

Here's a template for each of your entries today. Be sure to answer all of the questions above.

AFGO HOMEWORK:

Time:

Before eating:

While eating:

After eating:

What else did you notice today?

# DAY 5: FEELINGS, NOTHING MORE THAN FEELINGS

Today, let's get curious about what's going on in your mind when you're *not* eating. If you're new to "thought work" it may be difficult to "hear" your thoughts. If that's the case, ask your Self how you're *feeling*. Name the feeling, and then ask your Self *why* you're feeling that way. That will give you the thoughts being cranked out by your busy mind. Ideally, do this exercise every hour on the hour from the moment you wake up. There is so much to learn by doing this. For example:

Time: 7:00 a.m.

Thought: I am a hopeless mess.

Feeling: Sad/scared.


Time: 8:00 a.m.

Thought: I wish I didn't have to go to work.

Feeling: Resentment.

And so on throughout the day.

Be as clear as possible as you write down each of your thoughts. Label the corresponding feeling. Don't try to edit or censor yourself. Just observe your mind's activity and notice how those thoughts make you feel.

AFGO HOMEWORK:

Time:

Thought:

Feeling:


Time:

Thought:

Feeling:

# DAY 6: TO BELIEVE OR NOT TO BELIEVE

You may notice that even when you don't want to have negative thoughts, they still show up. We tend to want to push those thoughts away, but that never works because it's not the thoughts themselves that are the problem; it's whether you choose to *believe* those thoughts. If you believe a negative thought you will create a negative feeling and vice versa.

Our feelings drive our behaviors. Have you ever noticed how you hardly think about food when you're lost in something you enjoy?

Today, begin to "wiggle the tooth" by challenging the thoughts you think. You don't ever have to believe them. In fact, you'd be wise to challenge them all. For example:

Thought: I have no control when it comes to food.

Ask: Is that really true? Why would I choose to believe that thought?

> *Well, it's not like food is tying me up and forcing its way into my mouth, so, no, it's not true at all.*

Ask: Does this thought serve a useful purpose?

> *This thought's only purpose is to cause me anxiety and a sense of helplessness. It serves no useful purpose. (Good to know.)*

When we don't challenge our thinking, we keep believing whatever the mind tells us. This perpetuates the cycle of Cry-Eat-Repeat and gives us further proof that we "have no control."

AFGO HOMEWORK:

Thought:

Ask: Is that really true? Why would I choose to believe that thought?

Ask: Does this thought serve a useful purpose?

# DAY 7: DECIDING HOW YOU WANT TO THINK

You have the power to pick and choose the thoughts and beliefs that *serve* you. Just because you inherited a belief system from your primary caregivers doesn't mean you have to keep it. You can get a brand new one, designed by and for your Self.

Take time to ponder the thoughts you want to think. The thoughts you believe will create the life you really want. If you don't like the results you have, it's time to change the way you're thinking.

For example: "I will never lose weight permanently," might become "I am in the process of discovering why I eat when I am not hungry." The first thought is likely to keep you stuck in the cycle of Cry-Eat-Repeat. The second thought is likely to feel better and therefore inspire you to change your actions, which will give you an entirely different result.

Finally, for this week, notice if you are having thoughts like, "I'm not losing any weight" and "This is never going to work." This is your mind trying to pull you back into the old way of thinking. Say pshaw and move on; otherwise, you'll be back in stage 1.

AFGO HOMEWORK:

1.  How do you want to think about your body? Why? What thoughts would you have to stop believing about your body?

2.  How do you want to think about food? Why? What thoughts would you have to stop believing about food?

3.  How do you want to think about the person you see in the mirror? Why? What thoughts would you have to stop believing about your reflection?

4.  How do you want to think about your current weight? Why? What thoughts would you have to stop believing about your weight?

5.  How do you want to think about going on a diet? Why? What thoughts would you have to stop believing about diets?

6.  How do you want to think about fat? Why? What thoughts would you have to stop believing about fat?

# WEEK 2

# MAKING SENSE OF IT ALL

Your mind prefers predictability and habit. It's so much easier to just maintain the status quo. This is why we may say we want to change, but then leave it as just *talk*. We've got to put our walk where our talk is if we truly want to make change happen.

When your Child Mind is allowed to run on autopilot, you're going to get the same results, day in and day out.

For example, let's say you decide you want to lose ten pounds. You have the perfect plan that, if you follow it, would result in weight loss.

But you don't follow the plan because the thought of going on a diet is worse than the thought of sticking a fork in your eye. As a result, you don't lose the ten pounds. Instead of taking responsibility, your Child Mind just gets frustrated.

Makes no sense, right?

Except—it makes *perfect* sense.

Because, although you *say* you want to lose ten pounds, You are not in charge. You're leaving it all up to your Child Mind, and she has no clue about responsibility and delayed gratification. Those are for adults.

It's time to make room for your Adult Mind to take full responsibility for the way you *think*, how you *feel*, and everything you *do*.

# DAY 8: UNDERSTANDING WHY YOU EAT WHEN YOU'RE NOT HUNGRY

In order to understand why you eat when your body is not hungry for food, you have to slow things down—what you're *thinking*, how you're *feeling*, what you're *doing*—in order to get a clear snapshot of what's going on in your mind and in your body.

The best way to do this exercise is in real time, when you find yourself eating even though you're not hungry.

AFGO HOMEWORK:

1. What was the feeling that caused you to want to eat when you weren't hungry?

2. What were you thinking? What thoughts created the feeling you described above?

3. Was there a person, place, or thing—a triggering event—that set this Think-Feel-Do pattern in motion?

4. Why did you choose to eat?

5. Were you aware of the feeling you experienced *while* you were eating, or were you eating too quickly to notice? Or perhaps you felt like you had zoned out. Do you think you were on the plus side or the minus side of the Integrity Scale?

6. At what point did you decide to stop eating and why? What were you thinking and/or feeling once you stopped?

7. In the moments or hours after you ate, what did you think about? How did you talk to your Self?

8. Looking back, what feeling were you trying to avoid when you decided to eat?

9. What do you think (or fear) might've happened if you had decided *not* to eat?

10. What thoughts or questions come up as you begin to recognize this TFD pattern?

# DAY 9: WHAT HAPPENS IF YOU DON'T EAT?

Remember, as you do the exercises each day, it's important that you stay *curious* rather than resort to Self flagellation. The last thing you want is a backlash of overeating because you're upset about the way you've been eating. Besides, you promised not to do the flagellation thing anymore, remember?

It's so important to shine a spotlight on the times when you over-eat and, whenever possible, take note of your Think-Feel-Do response—and, equally important, the event that triggered the response. Those triggering events are your AFGOs. By now, you may be recognizing a pattern to your AFGOs. Brilliant! You will soon be able to spot those triggers ahead of time so that you can decide to—*not eat.*

AFGO HOMEWORK:

Notice a time when you want to eat when you aren't hungry and then—*do not eat.* Instead of picking up the cookie, pick up a pen and start writing down all the details of what it *feels* like to not eat when all you want to do is *eat.*

What is your immediate response when you contemplate not eating the food that seems to be calling your name? What does it feel like?

Why do you feel this way?

Are you relying on willpower to keep you from eating? Why? What does that feel like?

How long are you able to sit with the feeling of discomfort without eating?

Do you notice whether the intensity of the feeling lessens, and if so, how long does it take for that feeling to go away?

What did you feel afterward?

Why did you feel this way?

What did you learn about your Self by doing this exercise?

If you were able to complete this exercise, high fives are in order. This one is tough, but the more you do it, the easier it will become.

Repeat as often as possible.

# DAY 10: UNDERSTANDING YOUR THINK-FEEL-DO PATTERNS

Today you're going to pay particular attention to the times when you are *not tempted* to overeat and compare them to other times in the day (or the week) when you want to eat even though your body doesn't need food.

Describe the specifics of what you are doing, how you are feeling, the thoughts that create the feeling, and how effortless it feels to not eat when you're not hungry—and conversely, how difficult it is to resist food even though you are not hungry for food. (Grrrrrrrr.)

Document the two patterns, in detail, in your AFGO Notebook. Be specific, starting with a description of the situation and the time of day, as well as what you were thinking, how you were feeling, and what you were doing.

Remember, in each of the patterns you are *not* hungry, but in one you choose to eat and in the other you do not. Let's see if we can understand why.

AFGO HOMEWORK:

| Pattern 1 | Pattern 2 |
|---|---|
| Not Tempted to Eat/Not Hungry | Tempted to Eat/Not Hungry |
| Time: | |
| Think: | |
| Feel: | |
| Do: | |

Observations:

# DAY 11: KEEPING TRACK OF THE TRUTH

There are two ways you can react to what I'm about to ask of you: one response will come from your Child Mind—"But I don't wanna."—and the other will come from your Adult Mind—"I *am* willing to do this."

The purpose of this exercise, one that you will continue to do for the next thirty-one days, is to stop you from lying to your Self—from telling your Self "just this once" or "this doesn't count" or "this is too hard." That last one, especially—it's getting old, don't you think?

Today you will start to keep track of all the food you choose to put in your mouth. Scientific studies show that people who are trying to break old patterns of behavior (and create new ones) are better able to make lasting changes when they keep track of their habits.

Believe me, I understand your Child Mind's desire to want to push back—but you're not a child.

Besides, this is not that hard (don't fall for that mind trick), and even if it were, are you not worth doing hard things for?

Make sure to do this in real time. Do not rely on memory to record everything at the end of the day. It is imperative that you know how you're thinking and feeling whenever you decide to eat.

Tell the truth. There is nothing to gain by not telling your Self the truth. Notice if you are tempted to "lie" or "omit" a bite here and there. And notice that you notice, and then pretend not to. This is your Child Mind trying to pull a fast one on you—call upon your Adult Mind to think this through.

This is where the rubber hits the road.

Be sure to fill out your food journal (in your AFGO Notebook) *every* time you eat—even if it's one bite off your child's plate.

Here's the template for your AFGO Notebook today and *every day going forward*:

AFGO HOMEWORK:

Time:

Description of Food/Meal + Amounts:

Thoughts before, during, and after eating:

Feelings before, during, and after eating:

Be truthful. A journal that shows perfect eating habits won't teach you anything. This isn't about showing what a "good girl" you are. This is about getting to know the parts of you that you've been ignoring.

# DAY 12: PRACTICING CONSCIOUS AWARENESS... WITH INTENSITY

The point of the Dignity Diet is to bring conscious awareness to your eating patterns, and in doing so, to understand why you overeat. At first this is going to feel rather intense. That's okay. Don't forget, your weight is an AFGO—an opportunity to find out what it is you're trying to stuff down with food. Be vigilant because your mind is going to want to fake you out.

The reason it's been hard for you to understand why you are overweight, despite your strong desire to have a healthy, trim body, is because you are unaware of the thoughts you think and the feelings you feel whenever you eat for emotional reasons.

The desire to *not* feel a feeling is strong when we believe we aren't capable of handling it; food helps us not feel the feeling we so desperately want to avoid.

AFGO HOMEWORK:

Either in real time or from memory, recall a time when you ate *without Integrity*—e.g., you chose to eat when you weren't hungry, even though eating at that moment went against your priority of taking care of your physical health and/or losing weight.

What were you thinking and feeling at the moment you chose to, in effect, throw your Self under the bus?

I call this "zoning out" (also known as the Land of WTF) because it means that you were out of the Integrity Zone, beyond −2 or +2 on the scale, and unaware of what your mind was "deciding" to

do behind your own back. If you can, try to pinpoint your awareness level on the Integrity Scale.

Notice if you feel resistance to doing this, and find the motivation
to *do it anyway* by accessing your Adult Mind.

Think of this exercise as your ticket out of hell.

Don't forget to fill out your food journal.

# DAY 13: LEARNING HOW TO BREATHE

Can you eat and breathe at the same time? Don't laugh. I'm serious. OK, I'm having some fun with you here, but have you ever paid close attention to the way you breathe *while* you are eating?

Your breath has a lot to teach you about the way you eat.

Today, pay special attention to your breath—even when you aren't eating, but particularly when you are. It's also good to notice how you're breathing when you feel compelled to overeat.

Pay attention to the times when you feel like finishing the food on your plate (even though your body tells you it's had enough), or when you want to make a beeline to the refrigerator or pantry when you know you aren't actually hungry, and then *stop for one full minute* and count how many breaths you take and record that number in your AFGO Notebook.

AFGO HOMEWORK:

Time of day:

What I was doing:

Number of breaths per minute:

Is your breathing shallow?

Is your breathing ragged?

Is it fast?

How would you describe it?

How do you feel?

What are you thinking?

If you feel resistance in doing this exercise, or any of the exercises, just notice this and ask yourself why.

What are you telling your Self?

Also, don't forget to do your food journal entries!

# DAY 14: CATEGORIZING THE FOOD YOU EAT

It's important to distinguish the foods you eat in order to make sure you're eating a proper balance of high-quality foods that you enjoy eating as well as other foods that you eat purely for pleasure, regardless of their nutritional value (but always in moderation).

I don't think it's helpful to label foods as "bad" or "forbidden." What's more important is that you eat with Integrity—no matter what you're eating, whether it's chicken, rice, and broccoli, or a supreme pizza loaded with cheese and pepperoni. Eating with Integrity means you take responsibility for your food choices by paying attention to how you feel before, during, and after you eat.

We can categorize food in three ways:

1.  B-Food is food for your <u>b</u>ody; it's high-quality, nutrient-dense food that sustains and fuels your body— think clean, lean, and green. This is food that helps your body function at an optimal level.

2.  D-Food is <u>d</u>elicious food that you eat purely for pleasure; you love the taste, but it has little-to-no nutritional value—think French fries or lemon meringue pie or death by chocolate cake.

3.  C-Food is a <u>c</u>ombination of the above; it has both good taste and some nutritional value, such as whole grain pizza topped with a little cheese, maybe some meat, and some veggies.

Today, look over your food journal from the past few days and notice how much of the food you eat could be categorized as B-Food, D-Food, or C-Food. Make a list of the foods you tend to eat most and the categories they fit into.

AFGO HOMEWORK:

B-Foods:

D-Foods:

C-Foods:

Make a list of your Child Mind's favorite foods.

Make a list of your Adult Mind's favorite foods.

Which mind is in charge most of the time when it comes to the foods you choose to eat?

Are the foods you eat more or less likely to support your desire to lose weight?

As we wrap up our second week of the Dignity Diet, I remind you that the first three stages of weight loss are not the time for you to be trying to lose weight. Notice if your mind is still focused on how you can "hurry this up and start losing weight." That's the mind-set that got you here.

I encourage you to take this one step at a time—you might even want to go back and read the lessons in part 1 of this book. Done in tandem with the Dignity Diet, your chances of creating lasting change increase exponentially.

# WEEK 3

# CONTEMPLATING WHAT YOU REALLY WANT

Do you really want to lose weight? Or are there other things you want more?

Week three of the Dignity Diet is about contemplating what it is you really want as far as your body and your physical and mental health are concerned, and more importantly, *why* you want it.

Does it feel like love to want it or does it feel like fear?

There's a big difference between wanting something and *wanting to want* something. With the first one you're willing to take action because you know exactly why you want it, and wanting it feels like love; it makes you feel inspired. But when there is little if any motivation, let alone inspiration, then you just *want to want* it, you think you *should* want it, but in reality, you don't—you want it from a place of fear. Example: "I want to lose weight because I can't stand the way I look" is not likely to inspire you, from a place of love, to take the appropriate action that will result in weight loss. Instead, you will be motivated by fear.

Wanting to lose weight because you think you "should" is a recipe for *not* losing weight, because it's lacking two key ingredients: Dignity and Integrity, a.k.a walking the talk because you believe you are worthy of the highest standard of care.

For example, saying you want to lose weight because you want to look like some celebrity in a magazine is not really why you want to lose weight; it's because of how you *think* it would feel to look like that celebrity. We somehow think that all of our troubles will disappear along with the weight. Yes, you will most likely feel better when your clothes aren't so tight, but from an emotional perspective, if you're still *thinking* the same way after you lose weight as you did before you lost weight, you're going to *feel* the same way, too. In other words, everything else will still be the same—including your sad face.

This week, spend some time really thinking (and writing in your AFGO Notebook) about what you want and *why* you want it.

# DAY 15: SETTING GOALS

After struggling with your weight for so long, you may be thinking that setting a weight loss goal is a waste of time. You've started and stopped dieting so many times in the past; you may have even met your goal weight before, only to watch it slip away along with your resolve.

But guess what? You are exactly where you are supposed to be. Your path has brought you here, and you have an opportunity to do things differently this time.

Today's exercise is to think about the goal you want to achieve for yourself. Make sure the result you want is compelling and exciting, so much so that you can actually *feel* it in your body. For some people, picking a number on the scale will feel constricting, and for others, it will feel inspiring. There is no right or wrong way. Check that: there is only one "right" way to feel and that is L-O-V-E. (Yes! I know it's corny. Corny is awesome.) If you're not feeling it when you set your goal, IT'S THE WRONG GOAL.

Bottom line: whatever goal you set for your Self, it must feel like you've set your Self *free*. It has to feel good *now*. If setting your goal gives you a pit in your stomach, it's not the right goal for you.

AFGO HOMEWORK:

What do you want?

Why do you want this?

What does it feel like to want this?

Do you think you "should" want this and if so, why?

If you want this, why don't you already have it?

Whom or what do you blame for not having what you want?

Are you taking responsibility for what you want? How do you *know*?

Now—

Write a rough draft of the result you wish to manifest for your Self with regards to your weight. Include the result you want for your body, but also how you want to *feel* as you strive to achieve your goal. Include what you want your relationship with food to be like, what you want eating to feel like. Your goal must *turn you on* as you're writing it. This isn't about waiting until you lose weight to feel that feeling.

# DAY 16: CLARIFYING YOUR GOALS

Pull out your AFGO Notebook and let's take a look at the rough draft you wrote for your goal yesterday. Pay extra attention to what feels good about this goal and what doesn't feel good.

Notice which parts are *believable* to you and which parts still need work. Do you feel you can go all in?

Rewrite any sentence that doesn't get you excited and inspired to achieve the goal. Change the words, play with ideas, or crumple up that draft and start all over.

Once you've played around with your goal so that you're willing to put your whole Self in, "hokey-pokey" style, write it on a three-by-five index card (or several).

Read your goal card every day, as in, *every* day, and perhaps even three or four times a day if that's what it takes to keep you motivated and inspired to stay the course.

AFGO HOMEWORK:

When you read your goal, how do you feel?

Is there a way to tweak this goal so that it feels even better?

Write your goal on several index cards and strategically place them where you'll see them throughout the day.

Regarding your food journal, continue to make daily entries and categorize each of the foods you eat.

Do you notice a greater level of awareness when you're tracking your food? Any goal you hope to achieve requires your constant attention. The more attentive (conscious) you are, the greater your chances of success.

Write down your observations and compare them to your earlier entries.

# DAY 17: BRAINSTORMING

I hope you've made copies of your three-by-five goal card and strategically placed them everywhere you can think of: the refrigerator, the bathroom mirror, your wallet—on your dog's collar, perhaps? It's really important that you have your goal on display, especially for those times when you need a little motivation.

It's also crucial that you keep asking your Self why you want to achieve this goal and the feeling you get when you think about doing this.

AFGO HOMEWORK:

If you have any lingering belief that your happiness depends on losing weight *first*, your goal needs some tweaking. Your number one goal is to feel happy first. What would you have to be thinking to feel happy now?

Today's homework is to brainstorm the thoughts you would need to think, and *believe*, in order to create happiness now. Your happiness can't wait. In fact, your weight loss success depends on getting happy first.

Also today, continue with your food journal, and start tracking how often you eat while you're in the Integrity Zone. Notice that when you're in the zone you're more likely to eat according to the needs of your body and not at the whims of your mind.

# DAY 18: DEALING WITH OBSTACLES

OK, so you've set a goal. Now you're going to think of all the potential roadblocks that may arise to thwart your efforts to achieve this goal. The point is to create countermeasures for each and every thing you can imagine might get in the way of achieving the goal on your three-by-five index card.

AFGO HOMEWORK:

What are the things that you predict will throw a monkey wrench into your best laid plans?

What has held you back in the past?

What patterns have you noticed in your past behaviors that kept you from succeeding at your weight loss efforts?

What thoughts typically derail your efforts?

No matter how small or silly the obstacle may seem, note each and every one. Sometimes the smallest ones can appear to be the biggest in those moments when you begin to doubt your Self.

As they say, the best defense is a good offense, and you'll want to have an answer for any obstacle that may come your way.

# DAY 19: PUTTING COUNTERMEASURES IN PLACE

Yesterday you listed all the potential obstacles to achieving your goal. Today you're going to come up with a strategy to overcome each of the obstacles that might thwart your efforts.

It's important that you take time to do this exercise. Don't just go through the motions of what you think *might* work; get creative and come up with some new ideas for how to approach the obstacles in a new way.

How can you break down each obstacle in a way that allows you to overcome it?

For example, you may list one of your obstacles as going out in social situations where food is being served. You worry that you won't be able to stop yourself from having seconds or that the dessert will be "too irresistible to pass up." Knowing in advance that these obstacles have the potential to derail you from the plan, think about how you might handle each situation. These are your countermeasures.

AFGO HOMEWORK:

Obstacle: Going to a party and being tempted to overeat.

Countermeasures:

1. I will focus my attention on the people at the party instead of the food.

2. I will have something to eat before the party so that I won't be distracted by the food.

3. I will keep a glass of ice water in my hand as a reminder that the purpose of going to the party is *not* to eat (otherwise, just stay home and eat).

4. I will remind myself that food is just food and that my friendships are more important to me.

Do this for every roadblock that you can think of.

# DAY 20: MAKING A PLAN

You've set a goal; now it's time to make a plan. After all, a goal without a plan is a dream.

And we are so done with dreaming.

AFGO HOMEWORK:

Using the goal you have on your three-by-five card, which you've hopefully memorized by now, along with the potential obstacles you have identified and the countermeasures you have put in place, you are now going to write a detailed plan of attack.

Exactly *how* are you going to achieve your goal? What do you need to *do* to get this done?

What needs to change?

What will you commit to doing daily?

How will you keep yourself on track?

Make a list including the how, what, when, and where for each item on your list. For example, you don't want to simply write, "Eat healthy food," because there's no way to measure that. Instead you want to write precisely the types of foods you will eat. What are your breakfast, lunch, and dinner options? What will you have available for snacks? The more detailed the better.

The same goes for exercise: What types of exercises will you do? How often? Will you work out at a gym or with a buddy?

What is the minimum you will do to move your body? How many days a week will you exercise?

You wouldn't travel somewhere without knowing how to get there; the same goes for your weight loss journey.

Your plan is your map to where you want to go. Without it, you'll be lost.

# DAY 21: BRINGING INTEGRITY BACK

One of the biggest obstacles you're likely to face on this journey of Self discovery is the one created by your Child Mind. Yes, your Child Mind—a master at coming up with defeatist thoughts and limiting beliefs—can't wait to derail you.

You are undoubtedly becoming much more aware of the thoughts that tend to throw you off your game: "This is too hard." "I deserve to eat this." "I'll start tomorrow." These are the kinds of thoughts we have when we step out of Integrity. We've lost sight of our priorities. We've forgotten what matters most to us. After all, do your priorities only include easy things? What do you deserve more: A piece of cake or your precious health? Why would you make your body wait until tomorrow to take care of it?

Remember, when you are in the Integrity Zone you are in charge, in control, and at peace. You know what you want, and you're determined to get it. Child Mind doesn't live in the Integrity Zone—Adult Mind does.

Today you're going to put Child Mind in a (cozy and comfortable) corner so that Adult Mind can take charge. Use the Integrity Scale[3] to keep your mind from wandering off into the Land of WTF.

## The Integrity Scale: Measuring Conscious Awareness

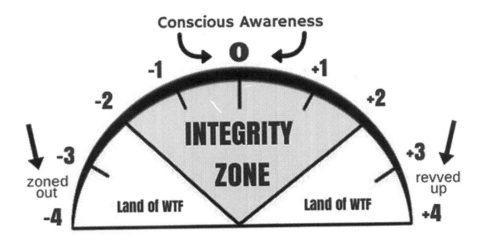

Today, make a list of the thoughts that you tend to *think without thinking*—subconscious thoughts that cause you to feel out of control and unsettled. See if your Adult Mind can hone in on those thoughts—they can be rather slippery—and then find a way to think yourself back into the Integrity Zone where you are in charge, in control, and at peace in your mind. For example, you may not be aware of how often you think the thought "This is too hard." It's often much easier to identify the feeling than it is to catch the underlying thought or thoughts that create the feeling. The way you're feeling (defeated perhaps) may be the first clue that your thinking requires some scrutiny. You'll need to call your rational Adult Mind into action in order to spot the underlying thoughts that cause you to feel defeated.

This is when you can counter the negative thought with "Maybe that's not true." If you're up for the challenge, see if you can then find proof that it's not actually "too" hard. When we're unconscious

---

[3] If you'd like to download and print out a copy of the Integrity Scale, visit www.LinEleoff.com

we'll believe anything our mind tells us. Getting conscious allows us to challenge every negative thought we think.

To clarify, it's not that I want you to think, "This is easy." I'm just asking you to *wiggle that tooth,* to challenge your mind a little, to see if there is a better, more useful way to think.

Sometimes even the slightest shift in thinking is all it takes to step back into Integrity.

AFGO HOMEWORK:

List at least ten thoughts that keep you out of the Integrity Zone. Put a number that corresponds with your (un)consciousness level beside each thought. (Remember, −4 means your mind has "zoned out" or "shut down" and +4 is when your mind is racing with thoughts.) Then ask, "What if that's not true?" See how close you can get yourself back to the zone.

And don't forget your food journal.

# WEEK 4

# WHY ARE YOU OVERWEIGHT?

Why do you think you are overweight?

I have heard many answers to this question:

- It's a way of protecting myself.
- My metabolism is slow.
- I'm going through menopause.
- It's my mother's fault.

Um, actually, none of these statements are true. The real reason you are overweight, barring any medical condition that goes beyond the scope of this program, is because you overeat for emotional reasons: in other words, you have extra weight on your body because you eat food when your body doesn't need it for fuel.

Menopause may make it more challenging to maintain a healthy weight, but if we use it as an excuse, we are not taking responsibility.

Diabetes may make it more challenging to maintain a healthy weight, but if we use it as an excuse, we are not taking responsibility.

Genetics may make it more challenging to maintain a healthy weight, but if we use it as an excuse, we are not taking responsibility.

Thyroid malfunction may make it more challenging to maintain a healthy weight, but if we use it as an excuse, we are not taking responsibility.

Remember the Dignity Sandwich?

Your beautiful body needs fuel to keep it alive. Your brilliant body sends you signals when it needs food—is that your stomach growling?

It'll also tell you when it's had enough to eat. But—

Have you been paying attention to your body's physical hunger signals, as opposed to your mind's emotional-hunger messages?

Do you trust your body's hunger signals?

Or have you forgotten what real physical hunger feels like?

This week we'll be checking in with your body to discover what it innately knows: how much food you *need* to eat.

# DAY 22: BODY WHISPERING—LEARNING TO LISTEN SO YOUR BODY CAN TALK

Today you're going to get acquainted with your body's built-in fuel gauge. It may take some practice, especially if you've been overriding your body's hunger signals for a long time. Or perhaps you forgot what physical hunger feels like because you've been taking cues from your emotions.

Understanding your body's hunger signals will help you pay attention—to really listen—to your body's "talk." Like Goldilocks, your body likes to feel "just right," which requires that you eat when your stomach is empty (but not starving to the point that it starts to eat itself), and stop eating when your stomach is full but not stuffed.

Why do we eat this way? Because it's the kind, respectful, loving way to treat your body.

Use the Dignity Hunger Scale[4] to help get reacquainted with your body's hunger signals.

## The Dignity Hunger Scale: Measuring Physical Hunger

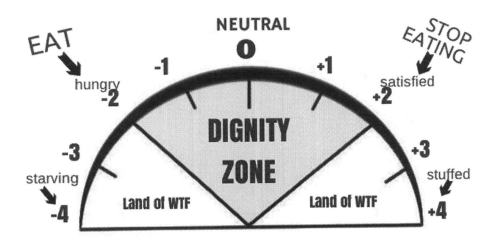

Your intention for today, and for each day going forward, is to eat with Dignity: feed your body when it's *hungry* and stop when it's *satisfied*. Do this because your body matters to you.

Remember: hunger is your body's business, not your mind's.

Today we begin exploring what physical hunger feels like *in your body*. We want to distinguish it from emotional hunger, which is all in your mind.

Listen for your body's whispers that it needs to be fed. Physical hunger is a feeling of emptiness in your belly. If you wait too long, you will push your body to the point of starvation, and that's when all bets are off—you're likely to make poor food choices and eat more than you need whenever your body starts to scream for food.

---

4  If you'd like to print out a copy of the Dignity Hunger Scale, visit www.LinEleoff.com

Eat when your fuel gauge reads −2. Stop eating when your fuel gauge reads +2. It's the *dignified* thing to do. When in doubt, have a Dignity Sandwich and a slice of Integrity Cake.

When you write in your food journal, make a note of your hunger levels before and after you eat. Pay attention to your thoughts and emotions while you are eating. Notice when your emotions make it harder to listen to your body talk.

AFGO HOMEWORK:

Continue your food journaling and also include the following:

Before eating:

Hunger level: −4 −3 −2 −1 0 +1 +2 +3 +4

Thoughts I was thinking:

Emotions I was feeling:

While eating:

Thoughts I was thinking:

Emotions I was feeling:

After eating:

Hunger level: −4 −3 −2 −1 0 +1 +2 +3 +4

Thoughts I was thinking:

Emotions I was feeling:

Also, start to really pay attention to the emotions that "feel" like hunger and the times when you want to eat when you're not physically hungry—name *that* feeling. Why are you feeling it?

# DAY 23: WILLINGNESS POWER BURNS FAT

Making the commitment to eat with Dignity and Integrity requires a willingness on your part to feel *some* discomfort as you learn to listen to your body. There will be times when your Child Mind will tell you to keep eating, even though you know your body has had enough.

This is a job for your Adult Mind. Stay curious and notice how your Child Mind will be having a hissy fit: it will really, really, *really* want you to go back to the old way of doing things.

Yes, this may be difficult. Child Mind is determined to make it so. It will tell you that you're suffering. Now's a good time to ask your Adult Mind, "If my body is telling me I've had enough to eat, what makes me think I'm suffering?"

Embrace it. Welcome it all. Then watch your Self handle it. Write about it.

Incidentally, if you've been using your AFGO Notebook to do this work every day, notice how much of the weight that's been in your head has been dumped into your journal. Your AFGO Notebook is a fat burner in more ways than you know.

AFGO HOMEWORK:

Do you notice any feelings of willingness or resistance?

What thoughts create the feeling of willingness?

What thoughts create the feeling of resistance?

Continue to keep track of your eating and your hunger levels before, during, and after you eat.

# DAY 24: WHY CRYING, EATING, AND REP*EAT*ING IS SOOOOO YESTERDAY

Eating with Integrity is the key to losing weight.

Let me repeat that: eating with Integrity is the key to losing weight.

Eating with Integrity is the backbone of the Dignity Diet.

Make a copy of the Integrity Scale, and keep it with you while you're eating to help keep your mind focused on walking your talk.

The Cry-Eat-Rep*eat* cycle is your Child Mind's clever way of avoiding responsibility at all costs.

This is why you need to pay extra attention to the thoughts that you've been allowing to roam free in your head: your thinking is blocking you from success. Be vigilant about writing down the thoughts that cause you to turn to food when you are not hungry and explore the TFD patterns that led you there. Remember, we're trying to get to the root cause of why you overeat; we're not looking for a quick fix, because there isn't one. If there were, you surely would've found it by now, right?

AFGO HOMEWORK:

Ask your Child Mind what it's feeling when you get stuck in the Cry-Eat-Rep*eat* cycle.

Where does Child Mind always seem to want to go?

What does it need from your adult Self?

How might Adult Mind help break the cycle?

What dignified thought could you think to remind yourself that you are a full-blown adult with more power than you can imagine?

# DAY 25: MAKING PEACE WITH ANXIETY

Anxiety is a signal that your Child Mind is in desperate need of attention.

Anxiety is an AFGO that keeps on giving and giving and giving.

*Note: Anxiety, as described in the context of this book, does not include generalized anxiety disorder, a clinical medical diagnosis best treated by a doctor. I am not a doctor and do not intend to treat any type of medical/emotional disorder with the information contained in this book. If your anxiety falls into this category, the discussion included here is not intended to replace medical treatment or go against the advice of your doctor.*

Anxiety is a state of turmoil in the mind and one that we've all experienced at various times in our lives. In order to make peace with anxiety, we must first understand its underlying emotions. You see, "anxiety" is a blanket term for emotions that rile up the mind. Anxiety is your mind's way of covering up feelings you don't want to feel.

Understanding the nuances of your emotions will help you determine how to best take care of your Self.

AFGO HOMEWORK:

What is it you really need in this moment?

From what, exactly, are you seeking relief?

What feeling have you been using food to cover up?

This is when your Adult Mind can prove to be very helpful in dealing with your Child Mind's tendency to want to feed on its fears. Instead, invite anxiety to sit across from you (not beside you or on top of you). Let go of your fear of anxiety itself—allow it to be present while you become curious. Detach your Self from the feeling and observe your anxiety. What feeling is it covering up—boredom, sadness, loneliness, jealousy, resentment, anger? Why are you feeling this? How can you think about this situation in a way that takes care of you?

Write down the thoughts and feelings, and then notice how long it takes for the feeling to pass through you when you're not pushing against it, when you don't eat or otherwise try to distract your Self from *feeling the feeling*. Is it a minute? Several minutes? An hour?

Record your experiences in your AFGO Notebook. Write it all down—the good, the bad, and the *chocolate*.

# DAY 26: UNCOVERING THE *REAL* REASON WHY YOU WANT TO OVEREAT

Today I'd like to suggest something to you for those times when you have that overwhelming urge to eat and you are *sooooo* not hungry; your body's fuel gauge is at neutral or above, and yet the desire to eat is consuming you.

First, look at the food you want to eat but then step out of your mind and observe the things you are telling yourself about the food: "It will taste so good." "I need it." "It will make me feel so much better."

Now, imagine the moment just after eating the food: describe that familiar feeling you get immediately after eating the food you desire so much. Is it relief? Satisfaction? Would you say you feel fulfilled? Is it a peaceful feeling? I'm talking about the good feeling emotions that come just after eating and *before* thoughts that create guilt and regret come flooding in.

Oftentimes, that good feeling lasts for a fleeting moment. We need to pay attention to it.

What *is* that good feeling? Because *that*, my dear one, is the reason you want to eat when you're not hungry. You want *that* feeling; you love *that* feeling. It feels so much better than the feeling you avoid by eating food.

In other words, you're looking for some sort of relief, and you've been getting it from food. It's a distraction tool that is counterproductive because it layers bad feelings (guilt, shame, remorse) on top of other bad feelings (frustration, resentment, anger) with just a brief moment of pleasure in between.

195

Not eating will give you so much insight into the feelings you spend so much time and effort avoiding. Today, step out of your mind in order to observe it.

AFGO HOMEWORK:

Answer all the questions listed above the next time you have an overwhelming urge to eat despite not being physically hungry.

# DAY 27: TAKING STOCK

Today we are going to take stock of your life: What is it like *without* food as a distraction?

What have you noticed so far?

Does it feel like you have lost or gained anything? I'm not talking about weight; I'm talking about your life. What, if anything, do you think may still be missing? Without food to distract you, is there a void?

Or is there an opportunity?

Do you notice any old thought patterns that trigger familiar feelings that drive the urge to overeat?

Maybe the old pattern was to deprive your body of food all day, only to overeat to the point of physical discomfort at night. What, if anything, is different today?

Perhaps you've noticed less physical tension because you're no longer white-knuckling your way to weight loss.

Perhaps you're beginning to notice less emotional tension when it comes to food.

When we don't eat when we're not hungry, we're more able to connect to the deeper parts of our Self that have been neglected and punished for so long.

There's still work to do, but hopefully you've cleared out some of the mind fat, which will make room for the emotional healing that remains.

Take a deep breath. You've worked hard. Keep going, my friend; because things are going to really get interesting as we move forward.

AFGO HOMEWORK:

Record your answers to the questions above in your AFGO Notebook.

And don't forget to write down what you ate today and whether you were in Integrity before, during, and after you ate.

# DAY 28: PROCESSING

Wow, you've been on the Dignity Diet for four weeks. Nice! Your Self thanks you.

Today we're going to take a look at your food journal for the past seven days. If you haven't been journaling for at least seven days straight, start today, and then come back to this page to answer the following questions:

How often did you eat with Integrity by honoring your body's hunger and fullness signals?

What kinds of food did you choose to feed your body? Why?

Do you ever have feelings of being deprived or anxious about food in any way? What are the thoughts behind those feelings?

Are you relying on your unlimited quantities of willingness power, or are you exercising willpower, a limited resource?

What's your energy level been like?

Hopefully this has been an extraordinary exercise in awareness. The more mindful you are of what you're thinking and feeling, the more conscious and deliberate you will be with the choices you make, and the more you will notice your inner strength.

Whenever you feel like you "have to" eat when you're not hungry, question that thought, and remind yourself how powerful you really are.

That power has been there all along.

AFGO HOMEWORK:

Answer all of the questions presented above.

# WEEK 5

# LET'S TALK ABOUT FOOD

I'd like to make something crystal clear just in case I may be giving you the wrong impression: food rocks!

Food fuels our bodies, it tastes delicious, it brings people together, and it has done so since the beginning of time. The Dignity Diet brings our thoughts about food and eating back into proper perspective.

As I like to say, food is just a bunch of ingredients in a bowl. And yet those ingredients can be crafted into works of art. But you don't have to consume food to appreciate it. You don't *have to* eat it. Eating it doesn't prove how wonderfully delicious it is.

As we enter week five, we'll explore your relationship with food. Note: this is not about judgment; it's about exploration.

# DAY 29: FUELING YOUR BEAUTIFULLY IMPERFECT BODY

Food's power lies in its ability to nourish and fuel your body. Of course, this is something you already know, right? But what do you *do* with that knowledge? Do you use it, or do you ignore it?

AFGO HOMEWORK:

What flavors do you enjoy most?

What foods have those flavors? Do these foods fuel your body?

What foods do you eat most often? Is it because they're your favorites or because they're just easy to prepare?

> Are they mostly B-Foods—the ones that fuel your body because of their nutritional density?

> Are they mostly D-Foods—the delicious but nutritionally void food you eat purely for pleasure?

> Are they C-Foods—those that combine good taste and nutritional value?

What foods do you crave?

> When do you crave these foods?

> Do you tend to resist your cravings or give in to them?

> Do you rely on willpower or willingness power to make your decision?

Do you deny yourself certain foods because they're "forbidden?" Why?

> What happens in your mind when you eat a food that's been classified as "forbidden?"

> Do you ever allow yourself to eat a forbidden food and enjoy it before, during, and after you've eaten it *without a side of guilt or shame*?

How do you eat food?

> Do you eat sitting down or standing up?

> Do you ever hide while you eat? Why?

> Do you hide food? Why?

> Do you feel shame when you eat? Why?

If you feel uncomfortable answering these questions, we're onto something. I urge you to not avoid answering these questions fully and deeply. Your responses are your truth, and we are done with hiding the truth, right?

And one more thing: these questions and the answers you give are not intended to give you another opportunity to beat your Self up. We are also done with Self flagellation, remember?

Be kind to your Self. She's on your side.

# DAY 30: ENJOYING EVERY BITE YOU TAKE

Imagine what it would be like if you only chose those foods that you truly enjoyed eating. No matter what you might choose to eat, your mission today is to simply enjoy every bite. After all, there is nothing to gain by eating food you don't like or eating food that is loaded with guilt, shame, and regret. That is *sooooo* not fun.

AFGO HOMEWORK:

Starting today, make it your mission to enjoy your food. *But* (you knew that was coming, didn't you?) before you eat anything, ask yourself these four questions:

1.  Is this something I would truly *enjoy* feeding my body?

2.  How will I feel *right after* I eat this food?

3.  How will I feel *at the end of the day* if I eat this food?

4.  Will it be *worth every bite* to eat this food?

Once you answer those four questions, then you can decide whether to eat or not. The goal is to make a choice that you are happy with—one you can live with.

When you're done, ask, "Did I actually enjoy eating this food?"

Do this throughout the day, each day this week. Remember, we are on a Heroine's Journey, and we've done a lot of exploring these past few weeks. Stay with me; this may seem tedious at times, but the alternative is a loss of focus. You're actually building new neural pathways in your brain as you learn a whole new way to think about food.

# DAY 31: THE TASTE OF DIGNITY

By now you should have a pretty good idea what Dignity "tastes" like. Can you describe it? Do you notice that you walk a little taller, perhaps? Or maybe you have a greater sense of resolve. Guard your Dignity, and make it a key ingredient in your life.

When it comes to food and eating, Dignity slows you down. It allows you to savor each bite of the food on your place. It is the antidote to a craving. By the way, have you noticed that when you crave something, you tend to rush? You may even feel a sense of panic. This is exacerbated by the belief that you "shouldn't" have certain foods because they're "forbidden."

When we think in terms of being "allowed" to eat some foods and not others, we are smack dab back in Child Mind.

AFGO HOMEWORK:

Today's practice is to give yourself permission to have whatever you want, as long as you do so with Dignity. Want a piece of carrot cake? It's entirely your decision, but whatever you do, decide with Dignity, and then eat the cake (or not) with Integrity. Where there is Dignity and Integrity there can be no guilt.

Make a conscious effort to *savor* your food today, tasting the Dignity in every bite. Dignity tastes like confidence and responsibility and resolve. If you can't taste Dignity, put your fork down and find the disconnect in your mind. Write in your journal. Pinpoint the thought that is coming between you and your Integrity. Guaranteed, it'll be a lie that your Child Mind is convinced is true.

How you eat is a pretty good reflection of how you live your life. Do you savor it? Or do you crave something more?

Get thee to thy AFGO Notebook!

# DAY 32: EXPLORING AND EXPERIMENTING

When you're deep in the throes of enjoying something, whether it's food or something else, have you noticed that your negative thoughts seem to vanish, and with them, the accompanying negative feelings? When there is gratitude and appreciation there is only peace and calm. Understanding exactly what it is you enjoy about the food you're eating, or contemplating eating, is all part of reclaiming your Dignity.

AFGO HOMEWORK:

Today you're going to put your Dignity to the test by savoring a food you love *without* eating it. Can you appreciate food without having to consume it? Notice that I'm not saying I want you to *resist* eating it; there's no Integrity in that. No, I want you to see if you can accept *not* eating something delicious and savor it at the same time.

By the way, this isn't something you want to do if your fuel tank is running on empty. We're not trying to taunt your body—we're just pushing the boundaries a little today.

The point is to keep loosening the grip that food has had on your mind. One of the goals of the Dignity Diet is to teach you that you've been telling your Self you have no power over food. That's just not true. It's one of the biggest, most fattening lies you've been using against your Self for a very long time.

OK, that was a lot of questions. Get to it, Mama!

# DAY 33: FOOD ASSOCIATIONS

Do you associate some foods with certain things? Do some foods remind you of people, places, or things in your life?

AFGO HOMEWORK:

Make a list of the foods you used to love to eat when you were a child.

Now make a list of the foods you love to eat as an adult.

How many of your childhood foods are still on your adult list?

Explore the associations you make with the foods from your youth.

Are there foods on the list that you associate with specific emotions or certain people?

Do you associate certain foods with "comfort?" Go a little deeper and find out what that's all about—describe what it is you're after when you're seeking comfort.

By the way, what does "comfort" actually feel like? Describe the times you tend to want to seek comfort in food. What are the patterns you notice?

# DAY 34: CAN YOU EAT JUST ONE BITE AND NOT WANT TO KILL ME?

Oh dear. You may not like today's assignment at first. Go with the flow—it's only for today. This is another one of those pushing-the-boundaries-of-the-mind kinds of exercises.

The idea today is to get a fairly large serving of a food that you absolutely love, love, *love* to eat because it tastes absolutely delicious. No food is off-limits. And no cheating—don't make this easy by choosing something that you don't really love to eat. It doesn't have to be expensive. It just has to be big and delicious. (One of my awesome clients, Bronwyn, did this with a *quarter slab* of her favorite chocolate cake—something she had been telling me was her "ultimate weakness.")

Next, (brace your Self) you're going to sit down and take just one bite.

Then, put your fork down and savor that one bite.

For some of you this will bring up a number of thoughts and emotions. It is most important that you allow those thoughts and feelings to move through you. Remain curious. Be a neutral observer who is merely amused by her own mind.

Whatever you do next, do *not* take another bite of this food, no matter how intense a feeling you're experiencing. Notice how this feeling *feels*, and notice the thoughts that go with it. If it's actual hunger you're feeling, notice that too. Don't worry; you are not going to die. But notice if you think you might.

Breathe. Watch your mind with compassion. After ten minutes, put the food away in a place where you can readily see it.

Next, pull out your AFGO Notebook and go nuts. Every time you see the food and want to eat more of it, write it down. What are you thinking? Do you believe your thoughts? How are you feeling?

Do this throughout the day. Eat your regular meals, but do not eat *that* food.

Then, at the end of the day, when you've recorded all the thoughts and feelings in your journal (including all those mean pictures of me), you're going to throw the food away in the garbage.

Oh no, I did not just say that, did I?

Um. Yes, I did. Throw it away. All of it. Don't take another bite. Don't put it away for tomorrow. Don't offer it to someone else.

THROW IT IN THE GARBAGE.

I know, this may seem very difficult and *wasteful*. Again, notice all the thoughts that come up—the thoughts about wasting food and the beliefs that drive those thoughts. Where do those beliefs come from? So many of us have been taught not to waste food. Better to eat it than to throw it away (apparently).

Dig in and catch those thoughts. How did they get there? Who first said them to you? What tone of voice did they use?

Embrace it all. Notice how strongly you may want to fight this. Do you understand why?

When I first asked Bronwyn to do this, she pushed back with a vengeance.

"Why would I do that? That doesn't make any sense."

"That's so wasteful? You're crazy."

But to her credit, she did it anyway, and this is what happened.

Bronwyn stared at the quarter slab of chocolate cake for the entire morning. After she had her lunch she sat down with the cake and had one bite. Then she watched all hell break loose in her mind. She sent me e-mails throughout the day:

First e-mail: 1:00 p.m. *This is a stupid idea. I had one bite. Happy now?*

Second e-mail: 2:15 p.m. *I keep staring at the damn cake. I feel like it's taunting me. This is dumb. I want to eat more.*

Third e-mail: 4:55 p.m. *What the f\*%$? I haven't eaten any more cake, but I feel like I'm going to cave, so I'm writing you this e-mail instead. Next I'm going to have dinner. We'll see what happens after that.*

Fourth e-mail: 7:05 p.m. *I can't believe I have not eaten any more cake. Wow. I'm impressed. But I think the cake is mad at me. It's giving me the stink eye. I know it can't talk, but I swear it's calling my name in a very eerie-sounding voice.*

Fifth e-mail: 9:22 p.m. *I actually cut a piece of the cake, put it on a plate, and just stared at it. I noticed I was actually afraid to throw away the cake, and I asked my Self why. After a few minutes, the* answer came to me: "It's because you might need the cake." Need? Cake? That's when I threw the damn thing out.

Wait. What? She thought she might *need* the cake?

In our phone call the following day, Bronwyn told me she was stunned when she heard her mind say, "Don't throw it out; you might need it." She hadn't even realized she'd had such a lame belief. To me it all made sense. Bronwyn's Child Mind had made an association to sweet treats like cake, years ago; cake, especially, had been filling an unmet need.

The unconscious mind works in very mysterious ways, and sometimes we have to resort to some crazy tactics to get at the truth.

The truth is very slimming.

Hark! Is that your AFGO Notebook calling?

AFGO HOMEWORK:

*Ridiculously Crazy Exercise:* Choose a generous portion of a food that you love, love, love to eat, eat, eat, and then follow the directions as outlined above.

# DAY 35: KEEPING AN OPEN MIND

Our focus this week has been on enjoying and savoring our food and noticing our reactions to cravings.

Have you managed to loosen the grip you may have had on some foods while embracing the taste of foods you might not have bothered to try? Keeping an open mind expands your world. As you keep your mind open around food and eating, you're more likely to open up your mind to other things in your life that have closed you off.

AFGO HOMEWORK:

In your AFGO Notebook today, think of ways you shut your Self off from trying new things or thinking about some things in a whole new way.

Be sure to give your Self a lot of time to process the work we did this week—you might discover many deeply held beliefs you've had about food: for example, that you must stay away from your favorite foods because they will "make" you gain weight. Perhaps you used to believe that food must be consumed in order for it to be enjoyed, that you mustn't have certain foods in the house because you "can't control" yourself. But none of that is factually true—it's just part of the story you've been telling for years.

My hope is that you're really starting to chip away at those old beliefs as you learn to savor your food and your life.

As you journal today, take special note of the old beliefs you've uncovered and any insights (new ways of thinking) you can begin to integrate into your life.

It's not always clear why we cling to our thoughts about food and other things, so hang in there, be patient, keep an open mind, and when in doubt, make a Dignity Sandwich.

# WEEK 6

# MAKING IT ALL STICK

I love this quote from George Carlin: "Just when I discovered the meaning of life, it changed."

The meaning of *your* life will be defined by all the beliefs you have gathered in your mind. You are a bundle of beliefs, many of which are secondhand. Some of those beliefs are awesome, and some are the direct cause of the extra fat on your ass.

Change your beliefs; change the meaning of your life, and, therefore, its reality.

If you've been following the Dignity Diet every day, doing all the exercises, and practicing new ways to think (I mean, really *think*) about food and eating and your body, you may be walking a little taller these days—and dancing a little lighter. Yes, you may have lost a few pounds, but I'm talking about that lightness in your step, that sense of "getting things done" because you're inspired and motivated. All that has happened because you shifted some beliefs around, threw out a few of the heavier ones, and lightened the load in your head. No wonder your body is lighter—you've lost weight in all the right places, not the least significant of which is your *head.*

As long as you stay focused on losing the weight in your head, the weight on your body will take care of itself.

As we head into this last week of the program, we'll be concentrating on ways to make your new Think-Feel-Do patterns stick as in, like Krazy Glue. Even though you may be feeling like you're on a roll, it's going to take a lot of practice to make these new patterns stick; there will be times when your mind will be tempted to take the path of least resistance. Creating a new path takes commitment to deliberate and conscious awareness.

Asking questions like, "How long is this supposed to take?" is not a good idea. It's going to take as long as it takes for you to stop asking that kind of question.

Here's a better question: "How can I make this last?"

OK—we're in the home stretch. Ready for a big finish?

# DAY 36: CREATING LASTING CHANGE

I know, I know, you want results and you want them now. Actually, you wanted them the day after we started, right?

But creating lasting change can only happen when you stop waiting for the change to happen. Waiting for change is a sign that you are resisting change.

What exactly is the change you are looking for?

What will it take to make it happen? This question requires your immediate attention. Look through your AFGO Notebook for clues. Go back to part 1 of this book, in particular stages 2 and 3, to read more about why you need a steady diet of Dignity and Integrity.

AFGO HOMEWORK:

Make a list of the patterns you want to continue going forward.

What things have worked for you the last five weeks? Take a look back in your AFGO Notebook and see which tools helped you the most. List them in today's journal entry.

Which tools did you find easy to incorporate into your life?

Which ones were more difficult for you and why?

This is how you set your Self up for long-term success.

# DAY 37: RE-THINK—RE-FEEL—RE-DO

The depth of your negative Think-Feel-Do habits will determine how long it will take to replace them with new and improved TFD habits that become part of your everyday life.

Today you're going to take an inventory of the negative TFD habits you've managed to turn into positive TFD habits so far.

What new habits and patterns are you still working to establish? List them in today's AFGO Notebook. What thoughts would you have to believe to turn those old habits into ones that serve you? Remember, you are a big bundle of beliefs.

The goal of the Dignity Diet has never been to create a tabula rasa—clean slate—in your mind. On the contrary, the goal has been to learn to question every belief that creates a painful thought in your mind. Remember, a belief is a thought that's had a lot of practice. You erode a painful belief by refusing to believe your own mind. When you refuse to believe a thought, the underlying belief on which it is based starts to erode. Sure, it may pop up from time to time, but it will no longer have the power to bring you to your knees.

In your AFGO Notebook today, identify an old Think-Feel-Do habit and the new and improved one you're creating.

AFGO HOMEWORK:

Step 1: I used to...

Think:

Feel:

Do:

The reality this TFD pattern created was:

Step 2: Now I…

Think:

Feel:

Do:

The reality this new TFD pattern is helping me create is:

# DAY 38: THE VERY FIRST STEP

*The journey of a thousand miles begins with a single step.*

~Lao Tzu

Let's talk about the Dignity Diet Exercise Plan, which can be summed up like this: Take. One. Step. Repeat.

Habits are born out of repeating the same Think-Feel-Do patterns over and over. To create new (dignified) habits and patterns that keep you in Integrity, it's best to start by focusing on the Very First Step. Not all the steps, just the Very First Step (VFS).

For example, if your goal is to get up every morning at six and walk three miles, starting tomorrow, you may have a hard time making it a habit, especially if you've spent the last six months doing nothing. There's a good chance your old thought habit of saying, "Forget it, I'll start tomorrow," will convince you to put off your walk. When you try to make a big change in what you *do* without first changing how you *think* and *feel*, your old TFD habits are going to trump your best laid plans.

If you want to change a behavior—the "do"—it's best to do so in incremental steps. It's easier to get your mind on board if you concentrate on the VFS.

Habits are thoughts, feelings, and actions that have had a lot of practice.

For example, let's say you want to start walking for exercise but you find it difficult to *feel* motivated. That's because of what you're thinking: "It's too hard. I can't be bothered. I don't have time." These thoughts demotivate us when it comes to exercise. But what if all you did was concentrate on the Very First Step and build from there?

## HOW TO CREATE A NEW EXERCISE HABIT WITH INTEGRITY

Four-Week Goal: Walk five days a week for twenty minutes.

Week 1: The Very First Step

The mini goal this week is to put your walking shoes on and walk out the door. Leave your shoes on for twenty minutes.

Notice, this week's goal isn't to go out and *walk* for twenty minutes, it's to (1) put your shoes on, (2) walk out the door, (3) don't take your shoes off for twenty minutes, and (4) repeat five times this week.

That's it.

I bet you thought the VFS would be to just get out there and walk. No. Unless your mind is screaming thoughts at you like, "Let's hurry up and get outside and walk. It's going to be awesome," which is highly motivating, you're going to have to come up with a VFS that you can truly buy in to. In this case, it's putting your shoes on (for twenty minutes), and walking out the door. What happens after that is entirely up to you. You can walk right back in if you want to. In fact, if all you do is put your walking shoes on and walk out the door only to come back in, your Integrity will be intact as long as those shoes stay on for twenty minutes; you will have kept your promise to your Self. You'll be *walking* your talk. (Perfectly placed pun intended). Of course, you can always do *more* if you want to, but the absolute minimum is to put your shoes on for twenty minutes and walk out the door.

Week 1 VFS = Put shoes on and leave them on for twenty minutes.

Now, how difficult will it be to motivate yourself to simply put your shoes on and leave them on, even if all you do is walk out the door and come right back in? You'll have a hard time convincing yourself that's too hard. In fact, you'll probably think it's too easy—and that's why it's brilliant.

Think: "This is easy."

Feel: Motivated.

Do: Put shoes on and walk out the door.

As long as your shoes stay on for twenty minutes, you can do whatever you want.

Week 2: The Very Next Step

The Very Next Step is to add another (very doable) step. This week you'll do everything you did last week *plus* walk for five minutes. This should be fairly easy after laying the groundwork last week. Walk out the door and keep walking for five minutes. Shoes must still stay on for twenty minutes, but walking in them is only required for five.

Week 3: The Step After That

Repeat the habits you established in weeks one and two *plus* walk another five minutes for a total of ten minutes of walking.

Week 4: The Big Finish

By now you've established a pretty solid foundation for a lifelong exercise habit. This week you will repeat the habits you established in weeks one through three *plus* you'll now be walking for a minimum of twenty minutes.

You can accomplish any goal when you break it down in this way. The key is to make each step easy, allowing you to stay in Integrity. Like Dignity, Integrity can be intoxicating.

Now it's your turn. Map out your Dignity Diet Exercise Plan in your AFTO Notebook.

AFGO HOMEWORK:

Four-Week Goal:

Week 1: The Very First Step

Week 2: The Very Next Step

Week 3: The Step After That

Week 4: The Big Finish

One last thing: your Dignity demands that you do hard things sometimes.

There's *always* an easier path. For example, I could choose to make my children microwavable frozen dinners every day, but I don't, even though it's a much easier option than preparing an entire meal. We tell ourselves things are hard as if that's an acceptable reason to not do something. It's not. You are capable of so much more. Besides—

Where's your Dignity, woman?

Programs that sell you on "easy" are capitalizing on your fear of hard. But really, what's actually hard about this? It's not that you have to go out and chop wood—and you know better than to believe everything your mind tells you, right? After all, this is not backbreaking work.

Committing to simply putting on your shoes every day for a week as the first step in developing a new pattern is not hard at all. This work—any work—only works if you do the work. If you've been journaling for the past thirty-seven days, keeping track of what you eat, savoring your food, focusing on your Dignity and Integrity, working on developing new patterns, and maintaining a level of awareness that keeps you focused on your Self and what you wanted when you bought this book, then you are one dignified woman.

# DAY 39: TAKING YOUR POWER BACK

One of *the* most important questions you need to know the answer to is this: "Why do I eat when I'm not hungry?"

As you now know, feelings drive our actions. You choose to eat when you're not physically hungry as a way to avoid a feeling. Food is a distraction from deeper issues you don't want to deal with.

That feeling you're trying to avoid is the reason you overeat.

Think about it: we overeat because we believe a thought that makes us feel an emotion we don't like feeling.

Think → Feel → Eat

"I can't resist this cake." → Powerless → Eat

"I have to lose weight." → Anxiety → Eat

"I don't know what to do with my Self." → Boredom → Eat

"I feel so deprived." → Resentment → Eat

"She makes me so mad." → Frustration/Anger → Eat

"I hate the way he treats me." → Helpless → Eat

"I'm such an idiot." → Ashamed → Eat

"I don't want him to die." → Fear → Eat

If overeating is caused by a thought that creates a feeling we don't like, it's important to slow down enough to find the thoughts and feelings that drive the behavior of overeating. In order to understand your own unique "thinking code," you must pay close attention to the things that aren't so obvious—you have to dig deep.

For example, you're at a party and you aren't hungry. Everyone is eating. You begin to crave the hors d'oeuvres being served. In that moment, what are you telling yourself? The craving may be uncomfortable, but you *know* you are not hungry. What is the struggle in your head all about?

If you eat, you will have turned your back on an opportunity to find out. You will have turned your back on your Self. You eat so you won't have to bother to feel the feeling caused by the thoughts you were thinking. You sell your Self out.

In effect, *in that moment* you are willing to live your life in an overweight body rather than "suffer" through an uncomfortable feeling.

Why do we give such a moment so much power? Why do we do so much to avoid a feeling?

What have you learned from moments like this over the past few weeks? What emotions have you avoided feeling? Why? Has being aware of this pattern helped to change your mind?

Welcome these moments. They are opportunities to practice a new way to Think-Feel-Do your life. The more you practice, the more comfortable you will be in those situations, and soon you'll be wondering what all the fuss was about.

AFGO HOMEWORK:

Here are some of the questions you should be able to answer by now:

- What does it mean to you to "have Dignity?"
- When are you more likely to eat when you are not hungry?
- What "triggering events" create a TFD response that typically ends in overeating?
- What countermeasures do you have in place when you're triggered in this way?
- How can you tell when you are in Integrity? What does Integrity feel like?

# DAY 40: WRITING A BETTER STORY

Earlier in this book (part 1, stage 4) we talked about how the mind loves a good story. If you haven't yet done so, write down your story, the one your Child Mind has been telling you for years. Don't censor anything; now is not the time to let your ego start calling the shots. Besides, this is for your eyes only, so don't hold back. If you've already written and rewritten your story, do another rewrite—it can always be better.

AFGO HOMEWORK:

Here are some questions to help you get started:

1. Who do you *think* you are? Since you're probably already onto yourself, it might be better to ask it this way: Who did you *used to think* you were?

2. What were you like as a child? Why?

3. What is the same or different about you as a child and you as an adult?

4. Describe your relationship with your mother. What things stick out most in your mind about her? What things stick out most in your mind about the way she treated you?

5. Describe your relationship with your father. What things stick out most in your mind about him? What things stick out most in your mind about the way he treated you?

6. If you had a close and healthy relationship with your parents, describe a difficult relationship you had in the past. Why was this relationship difficult for you? What did you Think-Feel-Do back then when you were around this person? Why?

7. What impressions do you have of yourself today? Where did you learn to think about yourself this way?

When you're finished, read your story back to yourself. How does it make it you feel?

Next, go back to your story and cross out everything that is not *factual*. Example, "My mother is seventy-four" is a fact. "My mother is a control freak" is not. If you can't prove it in court cross it out.

When you read your story now, with just the facts, how does it make you feel compared to the earlier version?

Finally, using Kat's story (discussed in detail in Stage 4) as an example, rewrite your story, releasing all the painful parts.

Write a dignified story, and read it to yourself every day.

# DAY 41: LETTING GO

Have you ever noticed that you cannot grasp and release at the same time? It's like trying to make a fist while letting go of what's in your hand. Likewise, grasping for a certain number on the scale *and* releasing fat from your body cannot happen at the same time. The energy of grasping creates tension and blocks the release.

Dignity allows you to let go.

Integrity keeps you from grasping.

Throughout this process you will release old thoughts over and over again. This will greatly impact the way you feel and the things you choose to do. Releasing what's in your head will also allow your body to release weight it no longer needs.

Releasing the weight on your body is not where your attention should be—that's your body's business; it knows what to do. The "hard" part is releasing the weight in your head: the negative thought patterns and belief systems that have kept you grasping for those size-four jeans while reaching for another bowl of ice cream makes for a very fat head. Your willingness to understand the weight on your body, how it got there, and why it managed to stay there will ultimately allow you to release it.

In the end, the weight on your body has been a call to action—an invitation to go on a Heroine's Journey into your Self.

AFGO HOMEWORK:

Today you become the heroine. For your AFGO Notebook's final entry, write a letter to your body. Tell it everything you have learned about your Self. Apologize (again) for the ways in which you have mistreated it. Rescue it from years of pain and anguish.

Call it a love letter. Make it good.

*My Dear Beautiful and Loyal Body,*

# DAY 42: SO YOU WANT TO LOSE WEIGHT? PROVE IT

In case you missed it, the purpose of the past six weeks hasn't been to get you to lose the weight, but to help you clear out the extra weight you've been carrying around in your head because that's the cause of the excess weight on your body.

Saying you want to lose weight is easy. Proving it to your Self takes guts and Dignity and Integrity.

Today marks a new beginning, my friend. If you have followed the Dignity Diet as suggested throughout this book, you cannot possibly be in the same place you were when you started. I would even venture to say you are a different person. You have done some thoughtful and powerful soul work.

Your life's *purpose* isn't to find something you love to *do*; it's to find a way to take care of your Self with Dignity and Integrity. Those are the key ingredients to creating a purposeful life.

But here's the thing—no matter what your weight is today, ask your Self this: Am I willing to prove that I matter enough to take care of my body?

Your bundle of beliefs created the body you have today. But if you've learned nothing else, I hope you never beat up your body again. You cannot beat your Self thin. If it were possible, you would not still be overweight today.

It is my hope that these last six weeks have set you up for the next six weeks and the next six weeks after that. As long as you're moving in the general direction of forward, you're making progress.

I encourage you to stay on your Heroine's Journey. I also hope that you can now see that your weight has always been an invitation to journey inside your Self.

Whatever it is you say you want in this life, I hope you're willing to *prove it.*

AFGO HOMEWORK:

Use this space to make a promise to your Self. What is your promise? (Does it feel like love?)

# CONCLUSION: GETTING YOUR ASS TO HAPPY

Here is what I believe:

Dignity is everything.

Find your Dignity. Hold onto it. Never again let it go.

That's how you get your ass to Happy. Happy is a place you create in your mind.

Everything falls into place after that.

It all starts with Dignity, baby.

Short. Sweet. Simple.

*This* is your life's purpose.

A steady diet of Dignity changes everything.

Every.

Thing.

# ABOUT THE AUTHOR

Lin Eleoff is prone to asking a *lot* of questions, which may explain why she chose careers in both journalism and law. These days she spends her time writing, speaking, coaching, and mentoring women on how to live a *gutsy glorious* life.

Lin is from Venus (aren't all women?) and is married to Stephen, who hails from Mars. Together they live in harmony in New England with their four children (who come from HD209458b, a rogue planet outside this solar system about 150 light-years from Earth in the constellation Pegasus), and Chewy, the world's greatest dog.

To access materials included in *The Dignity Diet*, or to learn more about Lin Eleoff and the coaching and programs she offers, please visit www.LinEleoff.com

Made in the USA
Lexington, KY
18 July 2014